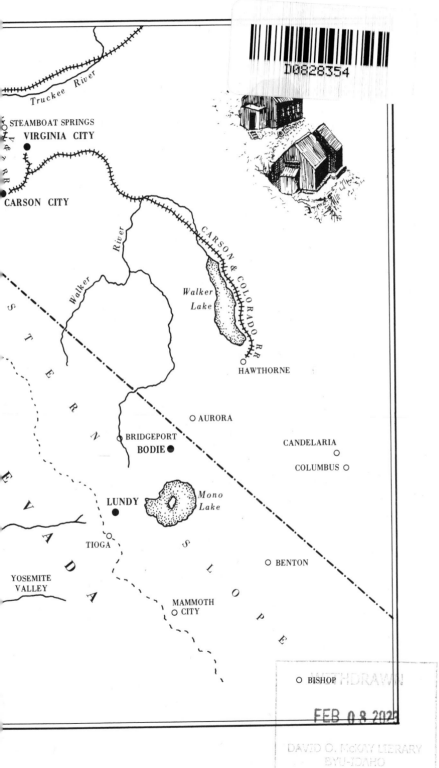

STEAMBOAT SPRINGS
VIRGINIA CITY

Truckee River

CARSON CITY

Walker River

CARSON & COLORADO RR

Walker Lake

○ HAWTHORNE

○ AURORA

○ BRIDGEPORT
BODIE ●

CANDELARIA
○

COLUMBUS ○

LUNDY ●

Mono Lake

○ TIOGA

S L O P E

YOSEMITE
VALLEY

○ BENTON

MAMMOTH
○ CITY

W E S T E R N   N E V A D A

Lying on the Eastern Slope

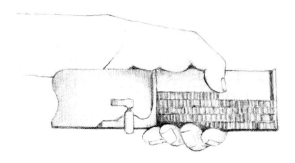

Lying on the Eastern Slope

James Townsend's Comic Journalism on the Mining Frontier

Richard A. Dwyer

and

Richard E. Lingenfelter

University Presses of Florida
Florida International University Press
Miami

Drawings by Larry Leshan.

Library of Congress Cataloging-in-Publication Data

Dwyer, Richard A.
  Lying on the eastern slope.

  Bibliography: p.
  Includes index.
  1. Townsend, James, 1838–1900—Criticism and interpretation.   2. American
wit and humor—19th century—History and criticism.   3. West (U.S.) in literature.   4. Frontier and pioneer life in literature.   5. Mines and mineral resources in
literature.   6. American wit and humor—19th century.   7. Tall tales.   8. Journalism—West (U.S.)—History—19th century.   I. Lingenfelter, Richard E.   II. Title.
PS3089.T48Z63   1984   813′.4   84–2251
ISBN 0–8130–0780–1

University Presses of Florida is the central agency for scholarly publishing of the
State of Florida's university system, producing books selected for publication by the
faculty editorial committees of Florida's nine public universities: Florida A&M University (Tallahassee), Florida Atlantic University (Boca Raton), Florida International
University (Miami), Florida State University (Tallahassee), University of Central Florida (Orlando), University of Florida (Gainesville), University of North Florida (Jack-
sonville), University of South Florida (Tampa), University of West Florida (Pensacola).

I had a dog that used to go out every morning after the carrier had passed and bring in the San Francisco *Examiner*. One morning he took it in his teeth and then spat it out and refused to bring it in. I suspected something unusual and went out myself and saw at once what was the matter. That paper had an article on the front page denouncing me as the biggest liar in America and the dog, being rather fond of me, resented it.

—J. W. E. Townsend

Contents

viii □ Contents

1

Introduction

SURELY humor is more to be savored than studied, but even
our pleasures, decently long after their taking, are as fit a
subject for investigation as any other aspect of human nature.
The trouble with initial gratification and deferred examination is
that there will be some catching up to do. As Walter Blair observed in 1937 in his classic study, *Native American Humor
(1800–1900)*, "A whole series of gaps . . . must be filled by other
investigators before a complete history of this important type of
American writing can be written." Even after the expanded re-
issue of that work and his subsequent *America's Humor from
Poor Richard to Doonesbury* (1978)—written with Hamlin Hill
—that statement still holds. It is truest, we think, in regard to

the humor of the western mining frontier.

Mark Twain's western writings have been thoroughly assessed, as have those of Bret Harte and J. Ross Browne, and a host of minor literary comedians and local colorists, from John Phoenix to Dan De Quille, have had their due; but important gaps in the study of western humor still remain. Neglected in particular has been the rich fabric of western comic journalism never collected into books. And the intricate fraternity of its makers has been overlooked as well.

What made copy for the editors on the mining frontier in the last century differed from what makes news for our big city journals partly in degree. Murder in the mining camps was as compelling and only slightly less frequent than it is in our unrenewed urban areas now. Advertising was less insistent, for the full-page spread had not been perfected. And crusades lacked only magnificence. Where a current metropolitan daily will indict abuses in clinical practice, a mining camp editor fumed at the dead hogs mysteriously piling up behind the Chinese laundry.

Often, however, the average frontier editor was left with several wistfully blank columns after he had set all of his ads and the clippings from his exchanges. Consequently, he was forced to create copy himself. The plodding and the prolix had little trouble in filling the gaps, but gave little pleasure by the result. A few newsmen, however, in a tradition that reaches "from Poor Richard to Doonesbury," let their imagination take the bit and run away with their credibility. Mark Twain, Dan De Quille, J. Ross Browne, Bill Nye of Wyoming's *Boomerang*, and even Fred Hart of Nevada's Sazerac Lying Club are familiar western examples of this persuasion. Familiar, because they have left their stories preserved between hard covers. Duncan Emrich rescued such others as Sam Davis and James Gally in his *Comstock Bonanza* (1950). Our worthy candidate for immediate resurrection from the ranks of the unbound is "Lying Jim" Townsend and our main purpose here is to give him a crack at his modest place among this humorous fraternity.

James William Emery Townsend (1838–1900) was a printer, editor, and recognized wit of the Nevada and eastern California mining camps during the last decades of the nineteenth century, and a good deal of his humorous writing is still to be found in the yellowing pages of the newspapers he published at such places as the river-delta farm town of Antioch, the sagebrush railroad stop of Reno, and the remote mining camps of Lundy and Bodie on the eastern slope of the Sierra.

Much of Townsend's reputation was as a talker, yarn-spinner, practical joker, public liar, and confidence man; a fellow one would like, from a safe distance, to have seen in action. When he came down out of the Sierra to the Comstock or the Bay, a crowd collected about him. And newspapers along the way reported his arrivals, departures and wisecracks en route. But the very impermanence of his best work—both that which has been lost in the air and that scattered among newspaper files—has led to what we think is an undeserved obscurity.

Our first concern, then, is to set before students and connoisseurs of American humor a selection of "Lying Jim" Townsend's writing that reveals him at his best. And two other concerns will lead us to broaden the canvas.

It was Townsend's fate to be remembered more for some of the stories told about him than for those he dreamed up himself. In part this is due to a curious feature of mining camp journalism, which we make our second concern in the course of this book: the fact that the editors of those papers formed a genuine fraternity of vagabonds who took a loving interest in each other's fortunes. Inasmuch as those fortunes were often sad or dull and those editors had reading publics to entertain, the reports they printed of each other were often sheerest blather. Townsend's own mendacity, of course, invited the inevitable; he became more lied about than lying. And those tales, often not as tall as his own, have tended by their number to smother the real details about his life. His true biography, then, will form our third concern.

Discussions of Townsend in our time have not taken up these editorial and biographical tasks. He remains anecdotal and mildly legendary. The stories related about him in Wells Drury's *An Editor on the Comstock Lode* (1936), W. A. Chalfant's *Tales of the Pioneers* (1942), Duncan Emrich's *It's an Old Wild West Cus-*

tom (1949) and in a number of magazine articles, of which the best is Howard K. Linder's "Dean of the Mining Camp Journalists" in *Desert Magazine* for September, 1961, continue to propagate the legends about him as the man who told Mark Twain the Jumping Frog story, as the model for Bret Harte's Truthful James, and as the publisher of a paper designed to swindle British investors. Interesting as these are, Townsend's own tall tales, "steamboats" as he called them, are more absorbing, and we are here assuming the task that he contemplated but never got around to doing: collecting his best stories between boards. Perhaps as importantly, we have tried to get at the curious character behind the tales, and at the eccentric circle about him.

To the end of placing Townsend in a legitimate perspective, we have set beside his own stories a few others by his fellow practitioners of what they called varnishing the truth. That craft they learned together as typesetters for such sophisticated papers as San Francisco's *Golden Era* and Virginia City's *Territorial Enterprise*, and they carried it with them to such dry backwaters as Benton, Mammoth, and Bodie. Orlando Jones, William Barnes, John Ginn, Robert Fulton, Ed Cleveland and others wrote lively copy about the camps, themselves, and each other, providing some deflating anecdotes about Lying Jim that are worth preserving.

There are things to be learned as well as enjoyed in the texture of this writing. In common with the humor of such colleagues as Dan De Quille, Townsend's employs the techniques of exaggeration, incongruous diction, *non sequitur*, and anticlimax, and his forms range from the one-liner through caricature and set-piece description to tall tales and semidramatic narrative. But here, we prefer to characterize his writing in terms of its medicinal functions. During one of his stands on the Reno *Gazette*, Townsend claimed to be working on a story called "Ten Nights in Jerusalem," which he proposed to illustrate with more than a hundred patent medicine cuts. The parallel between his prose and the snake oil pharmacopoeia is suggestive.

First, his stories are a tonic. His skewed view of such oddities of the camps as two cranky old bachelors making a 'Welsh rarebit' or the miners who cut out the use of tobacco with violent

results is fresh and invigorating. Other stories are useful anti-
dotes, especially to received history. Take the case of the Central
Pacific's connection with the Union Pacific in 1869, linking the
seaboards. While the schoolbooks say the railroad facilitated set-
tlement of the Far West and gave it access to markets, into the
amused view of our *Gazette* reporter it brought chiefly a stream
of dudes and ladies who would take four bites to eat a strawberry
if they thought anyone was looking.

What may be Townsend's best humor is antinaturalist and
antidote to the Golden Poppy school of the beauty of western
nature. Some literary historians have attributed the irreverence
of writers like Townsend and his fellows to a broad reaction to
the prevailing sentimentality of popular nineteenth-century literature. Many of Townsend's stories are complaint and satire
about the little irritations of camp life: mosquitoes, chiggers,
wood ticks, lice, and fleas. Under our noses waft the regiment of
bad smells a disorderly camp acquires. For him no stags pose
against the ruddy dusk; they are crowded out of the picture by a
horde of hogs, dogs, goats, rats, and reeking sheep.

As well as antidotal, Townsend's writing is purgative. He rails
at intruders on the mining scene: drunks, vagabonds, gamblers
and thieves, as well as lawyers, doctors and, above all, mission-
aries. What the mining camps need, he says, is not religion but
machinery and willing hands to work it. Finally, his medicine is
at times a balm. He can be a booster as well as a Jeremiah, and
what he praises is the wonder of wilderness. But the posture is
rare.

It should not be thought, however, that much of Townsend's
invention was intentionally therapeutic or, in fact, even harm-
less. He lacked, shall we say, Mark Twain's "moral vision." A
mild judgment might be that he was careless of ethical niceties.
He participated in a number of dubious schemes throughout his
career, misused his journalistic privileges, betrayed his friends
and subscribers, and funked other obligations in the course of
complaining about Mankind in print. And much of this caught
up with him as similar flaws had flown home to roost in the editorial rooms of his fellows.

Townsend's decline and fall started at two points. In the late eighties his health began to fail, and he was obliged to make several trips to San Francisco for surgery. His writing suffered too, as more and more energy needed to be spent in mere compilation of necessary and unvarnished news. A second, more interesting, cause for his retirement is veiled in the mystery surrounding a major mining scandal of the late 1880s. Townsend apparently shared in the culpability for which promoters of the May Lundy mine were indicted. But it is time to get on with it. The details of this and many another tale await.

2

King of the Cannibal Islands

*J*IM TOWNSEND made himself up as he went along, composing himself, so to speak, on the typesetter's stick. One summer day in 1859 he turned up on San Francisco's Clay Street at
the office of a little literary magazine, the *Golden Era*, asking to
speak with the foreman of the printing plant. As he was ushered
past the editorial cubicle where the owners, Rollin Daggett and
J. Macdonough Foard, played seven-up and wrote filler with a
pair of scissors, he remade himself for a job.

Lean, erect, and wise, he introduced himself as Jim Townsend, forty-six, a deft compositor of profound experience. A per-
sistent feature in his self-recreation was Townsend's lying about
his age. In truth, James William Emery Townsend was barely
turning twenty-one. Born to Anna and Richard Townsend in

Portsmouth, New Hampshire, on the fourth of August, 1838, he was the last of their three sons. The father was a merchant sailor, whose tales of the sea and foreign shores Jim later inflated and passed off as his own.

Townsend lived in Portsmouth his first nineteen years, and decades later reminisced with his brother—in the sentimental mode he usually scorned—concerning

those we knew when we were darling young boys together, and went to good Master Hoyt's school with a clean 'tire every day—the days when the big girls used to take advantage of our innocence and smother us with kisses every chance they got. (Why don't they do it now?) . . . Oh, yes—we raked the old town, and set fire anew to the schoolhouse, and recalled the time when brother John shot Cushing's geese, while John Frances held a lantern; when we used to steal hot buns from Uncle Bob's bread-wagon—he was a nice old pill, he was; he used to daub his horse's nose with gruel, and then hold a looking glass up before him, to make him think he had been eating meal. The worst clip of all was the intelligence that our old sweetheart had got married; she couldn't wait any longer for us to make a pile, and therefore took up with a fellow who meant business. We are jealous of that chap. All our dreary midnight tramps from Sagamore availed us not. Well, we will wait for the widow.

Despite his feeling for the sea, neither Jim Townsend nor his brothers turned to it for a living. His older brother, John, became a carpenter, Henry a baker, and at fourteen Jim apprenticed to a printer. He quickly mastered the trade but, by the financial panic of 1857, felt that he had done Portsmouth and was restless to make his fortune elsewhere. He signed up on the crew of a sailing ship, but whether he came straight around the Horn to California to try his luck in the Southern Mines of Tuolumne County, or spent a year or two following the winds, we don't know. In either case he appeared in San Francisco in 1859 eager to work as a printer.

The West Coast was slow to recover from the panic of '57, and those who had come there to find better times met only disillusionment. Unemployment was still wide-spread. Less than half of the members of San Francisco's Eureka Typographical Union had steady work, while the rest barely got by as "stand-ins" for those with regular jobs. Most of the papers in the city were staffed with older men who had come to the coast in the early fifties and now held their positions by seniority. But one paper that did hire younger men, the *Golden Era*, whose owners had been just twenty when they founded the paper in 1852, gave Jim Townsend a type case, despite his lack of experience and pretensions to the contrary. Here Jim Townsend set type beside such later notables as Bret Harte and Joseph T. Goodman and Denis McCarthy, who would buy *The Territorial Enterprise*. All were within a year or two of his own callow age.

Some of the printers on the *Golden Era* occasionally contributed poems and prose to the paper, but only if they had incandescent literary ambition—the owners paid nothing for poems and only a pittance for a column of prose. Apparently Townsend abjured this sport, or chose an unidentifiable pen name. Instead he spent his spare time treating the alley to tales of absurd or hair-raising adventure, often in the currently popular genre of South Seas yarns. One of these first stories was preserved by Jared Graham, one of Townsend's captive audience of "typos."

While on another alleged whaling voyage, this time in the south seas, his vessel was wrecked near one of the Fegee islands, and he with five other tars was rescued by the natives. They had not yet been converted from the broiled missionary habit, and after a protracted counsel decided upon having a grand feast at every new moon so long as the sailors lasted. The unfortunates were placed in a pen, and every month Jim saw the fattest of his comrades led away to the music of kettle drums, until he only remained. He was a skinny, lantern-jawed New Englander, so he had the rest easily scooped for last place.

When at length his turn came, the king appeared, preceded by drums and followed by half-a-dozen islanders in single file.

They felt of Jim's ribs with a no-good grunt but opened the pen and he saw that after six-months weary wait it was all off with him.

The king was togged out for a grand wind-up, and would brook no delay. He had on an extra coating of paint, a missionary's plug hat and a red necktie, which was all the clothing in the crowd except the rings in their ears.

In the return procession Jim was placed immediately behind the king. It seemed a cinch, he said, that he would be next to the fire in a few minutes, so for a parting diversion and to stretch himself after the long confinement he sprang to the side of the king, gave him a high sign and began a series of grotesque postures and kowtows that paralysed the islanders, ending with a salaam to the cardinal points of the compass. Then he handed the king a plug of tobacco, that he had concealed under his shirt though he did not use the weed.

Hiding that tobacco was the luckiest move Jim ever made. The mere sight of it electrified, for his benighted captors had learned that to eat flesh saturated with tobacco meant deathly sickness. The king rolled his eyes skyward and gagged; then they all gagged.

After a consultation, all meanwhile eyeing Jim with loathing, he was returned to the pen innocent of what was the matter.

Next morning, however, he was taken before the king, who by signs gave him to understand he was an immune, being no good for culinary purposes. It seems, too, the king had taken a great shine to Jim on account of his graceful posturing and gall. It ended by his being adopted by the islanders and forced to marry one of the king's daughters—with the view, he presumed, of improving the breed. Finally he was made the king's viceroy, or something like that, and he said he might have lived there happily ever after but for having made his escape on an English brig that touched the island for water.

Looking backward from the 1920s, William Gillis similarly recounts one episode of Jim's South Sea tale, in which he was trapped and forced to marry two hundred Amazons on a lonely desert island—escaping, only after he had wasted to a shadow, by jumping into the air to be borne aloft upon the winds for many miles out to sea. There he had the good fortune to hook a shark and ride him bareback at a frightening clip to the nearest land—whence, with the aid of an educated parrot, he found his way back to civilization. Of Jim Townsend, Gillis concluded, "He was one of the best story-tellers I ever listened to. Had his adventures on land and sea, his miraculous escapes from impossible situations, and many other hair-raising tales of escape from disaster and death, been published, he would to-day, instead of being dubbed the greatest liar in the world, be considered one of the greatest humorists who have filled the world with smiles."

In about April of 1860, Francis Bret Harte took a case on the *Golden Era*—on the rebound from his brief and unpopular career as editor pro tem of the *Northern Californian*, published in the coastal town of Arcata. Harte was no typesetter, nor was he happy in the position, and he quit the following year to take a job as clerk in the U. S. Surveyor General's office. Nonetheless, for almost a year Jim Townsend and Bret Harte worked on the same alley, and during this time Townsend is alleged to have so impressed Harte with his repertoire of tall tales and witty vernacular that Harte later modeled after him one of his most popular poetic characters, "Truthful James." The principal authorities for this identification are William, Jim, and Steve Gillis, all close associates of Harte and Townsend at the time. The case is argued most avidly by Robert Fulton, a later friend and admirer of Townsend. Although Jim Gillis, in particular, had been named as "Truthful James" by others, he firmly disavowed it in Townsend's favor. Richard O'Connor, a recent biographer of Harte's, accepts the attribution to Townsend without citing authority. Whether Harte did in fact have anyone in mind when he put "plain language" into the mouth of "Truthful James" is questionable—for he certainly never claimed to. And in either case, whatever popularity Townsend later gained in no way sprang from his identification as "Truthful James"—to be sure he never claimed the honor.

IN JULY of 1860, having sold the *Golden Era*, Rollin Daggett and Macdonough Foard joined partnership with a printer named

Rutherford to found a rival news and literary paper, the *Evening Mirror*. At first it flourished, supported by large advertising contracts with the city. But, with the looming of the Civil War, Daggett sought to take a strong editorial stand. His partners disagreed and backed out. The *Mirror* struggled on into the fall of 1861, when, lacking even the money to pay its printers, it faced suspension. At this time, Townsend with half a dozen other printers rescued it by contracting to publish the paper for several weeks in return for city scrip.

In this group Townsend met for the first time a bantamweight printer from Indiana named Orlando Ezra (Dan) Jones. On and off for the next thirty years, Jim and Dan knocked around the newspaper printshops and editorial rooms of the interior mining camps as close friends. Jones, six years Townsend's senior, had crossed the plains to Oregon in 1848 and worked as a printer and reporter on the *Oregonian* and other papers in the Northwest. Under the name of Dan Conover he had also toured the coast with a circus as a Shakespearean clown and jester.

Though he had been a clown on the road and a jester in print, Orlando Jones drank in earnest. And his drinking invariably interfered with his keeping a job—for he would work a few days and then drink for a few weeks, until he was known to every foreman on the coast as a pathetic case. But drunk or sober he was a very colorful editorial writer and conversationalist, and this alone endeared him to almost everyone he met.

As a violent secessionist Jones also acquired the nickname of Warhorse, but the one thing that Warhorse feared more than Union was smallpox. He lived in morbid fear of it, a terror that amused his comrades and once was rather cruelly used by Jim Townsend. Jared Graham, who was working on the *Mirror* at the time, recounts the incident.

Townsend was something of a practical joker, too. I recall one of the funniest things he ever perpetrated, though it had a singular and serious ending.

Once after a prolonged spree Jones staggered into the office in a shaky condition, his face spattered with mud from the wheels of some vehicle. Townsend, at the deadstone about to lift a handful, suddenly struck an attitude of fright and yelled:

"Great God! Warhorse, what's the matter with you?"

Jones turned pale but reckoned he was only feeling bad for want of a drink.

"Drink!" exclaimed Jim, backing away. "Why man, you're all broke out with smallpox. Look in the glass."

Across the office was a mirror, and in it Jones caught a glimpse of his soiled face. Uttering a cry of terror, he leaned against the deadstone for support. Jim then edged up a little and said compassionately, "Now, Warhorse, listen: Don't you lose a minute in getting to the hospital. You'll give us all a dose if you don't light right out. If you're too sick to walk I'll send for a dray."

Jones then braced up, and without a word staggered out the door. Several days later word came from the pest house that he was there so badly disfigured with pustules his intimate friends would not know him. In fact he went through every stage of the disease and came near dying.

The case caused much comment among physicians, and was the subject of a lengthy article in a medical journal bearing on similar phenomena. His doctor decided that he had simulated the disease through abnormal fear, and in fact did not have smallpox at all.

Those doctors might have been intrigued too by the fact that this episode marked the beginning of a lifelong friendship between the two men, a subtle and poignant bond.

In all, the *Mirror* proved to be a fiasco. When the contract was up, the paper folded and the printers were given the unredeemed city scrip. The foreman, Tom Bail, was elected to hold the scrip and try to lobby a bill through the state legislature authorizing the city to cash it in a lump sum. After several weeks of waiting, Bail went to the city treasurer and, cashing in all of the scrip he could, took the balance with him and caught the first steamer to Portland.

Townsend, Jones, and the others never saw Bail again and never got a cent for their work, but they did take a rude solace in hearing that he had been skinned of most of their wealth in a poker game and in a fit of despondency had hanged himself in Boise City.

3

Dirty Scamp and Miscreant

L IVELY' is a limp and soggy adjective to use as a prefix to Virginia City in 1862–3," wrote Townsend. "Forty thousand Leadvilles, Wood Rivers and Tombstones boiled down to a corner lot would be like a second-hand graveyard in comparison. The town was submerged in a tidal wave of $20 pieces, and an unbroken stream of silver extended from the Gould & Curry mine to San Francisco. In those days when a Washoite went to San Francisco, he chartered a theater, had programmes printed on white satin, and invited the universe. When he went on a spree he bought a distillery. When funds got low, he would slip into the *Enterprise* office and get Sam Martin to print a lot of Kenosha, Pewterinctum or Daly stock and sell it on the 'Washoe Board.'" So stood the boom when Townsend arrived on Sun Mountain in the fall of 1862.

The rush to Washoe was depopulating the mining camps of the Mother Lode and the towns and cities all along the Coast. Early in the rush Joe Goodman and Denis McCarthy had quit the *Golden Era* and come to Virginia City to purchase its only paper, the *Territorial Enterprise*, in March 1861. Swept up with the boom and backed by such literary talent as Dan De Quille and Mark Twain, the paper soon became one of the most popular and oft-quoted on the Coast—its subscribers ranging from austere prospectors on the Nevada desert to habitués of the lavish literary parlors of San Francisco and the investment houses of London. In six months it grew from a weekly to a daily, and its printers were among the highest paid in the country.

In spite of the paper's far-flung and sophisticated audience, the office of the *Enterprise* was small and primitive. The one-story frame building had a shed on one side, which had been "fitted up as a kitchen and dining and lodging place. Bunks were ranged along the sides of the room, one above another, as on shipboard, and here editors, printers, proprietors, and all hands bunked after the style of the miners in their cabins. A Chinaman, 'Old Joe', did the cooking, and three times each day the whole crowd of newspapermen were called out to the long table in the shed to get their square meal. The devil went for numerous lunches between meals, and often came flying out into the composing-room with a large piece of pie in his mouth, and the old Chinaman at his heels."

Possibly through his acquaintance with Goodman on the *Golden Era*, Townsend was given a case on the *Enterprise*. Here during stand-ins he had the opportunity to swap yarns with the paper's two local editors, Dan De Quille and Mark Twain—the latter having just hired on after a short fling at prospecting in Humboldt and Esmeralda. It may have been Twain's and De Quille's none-too-exaggerated tales of the wondrous country around Mono Lake, "the Dead Sea of California," that first sparked Townsend's interest in that region where he was to spend the last twenty years of his life.

As he acknowledges in *Roughing It*, Mark Twain learned from Townsend the story of "The Trestlework Tunnel" and at this time is also said to have got from him the yarn which he later made famous as "The Celebrated Jumping Frog of Calaveras County." Although this assertion is graciously attributed in Townsend's obituaries to Dan De Quille, Alf Chartz, and others who were on the Comstock at the time and is supported by Effie Mona Mack, it is really neither verifiable nor relevant. For even if Townsend did tell the story to Twain, it was by no means original with him, since, as Oscar Lewis has shown, it had been kicking around as fourth-page filler in the Mother Lode newspapers at least a full decade earlier. Thus it was already part of the general folklore when Twain recorded it in his notebook in 1865, and its popularity drew not from any novelty in its plot but from Twain's own colorful redaction.

Nonetheless, during the year or so that Townsend was on the *Enterprise,* he and De Quille, Twain, Goodman, Gillis, and others of the Washoe newspaper fraternity engaged in many bull session exchanges of yarns and witticisms that whetted and tempered the talents peculiar to each. This brief association served as Humour's Apprentice School where each pupil perfected his variation on the deadpan delivery of non sequitur and anticlimax and acquired a professional respect for his fellows' mendacity.

But everyone at that time was itching to be on the move, and in the winter of '63–64 Jim quit the *Enterprise* to work for the rival Virginia City *Daily Union.* Mark Twain and Steve Gillis quit the *Enterprise* and Virginia City the following spring—Twain to rise to fame and Gillis to return in a year or two. A year later Denis McCarthy sold out his half-interest in the paper to Goodman, and, with a sizable fortune for a man still in his early twenties, retired to San Francisco to increase it on the stock market. Against his hopes, in four short months he lost the entire gains of the previous four years, and he returned to Virginia City to become foreman in what had been his own job office. Goodman sold out ten years later and only Dan De Quille stayed with the old paper until shortly before its demise, reigning as its prime source of vigor and wit for the next third of a century.

While he was on the *Union,* Townsend got married. The event seems to have had little influence on his life, for the marriage record in the Lyon County Court House is the only document that mentions either the event or the lady. On May Day 1864,

Jim wed Elizabeth J. Lindsey at Dayton, Nevada, and six months later their separation was noted in the *Nevada Daily Gazette*. In his last years, Townsend is said to have lived briefly with a daughter in Oakland, but this issue is so obscure that we leave it up in the same air that he did.

On the *Union* Townsend rejoined three of his San Francisco cronies, Dan Jones, William W. Barnes, and Jared B. Graham. But their association was to be brief, for each was beginning to feel flush and eager to try his hand at publishing—perhaps inspired by Joe Goodman's good fortune. In August, Barnes led the way in an abortive effort to deliver a daily paper at Carson City. The following spring Jones proved more successful, after purchasing a part-interest in the *Union* to become its editor. But before this, Townsend had set out in a disastrous partnership with a Comstock hostler, Henry M. Blumenthal, to found a campaign paper at Grass Valley, California.

THE POLITICAL campaign of 1864 was one of the most heated in the history of the nation, manifesting all the violence and discontent of a nation in the teeth of civil war. Occasionally freedom of the press was completely abolished, as Union mobs, soldiers, and law officers alike burned and sacked newspaper offices, arrested and imprisoned editors branded as Copperheads. In some localities, however, the Copperheads held a majority, as they did at Grass Valley, then known as the "Charleston of California." Here, John Rollin Ridge, a fiery, New England-educated, part-Cherokee from Georgia, held the editorial tripod of the *Nevada National*, making it one of the most vitriolic and outspoken Democratic organs in the West.

Ridge was a prolific and accomplished writer, who, under the pen name of "Yellow Bird," warbled a steady stream of poems for California's early literary magazines and in 1854 created western legend with his book, *Life and Adventures of Joaquin Murieta, the Celebrated California Bandit*. Also, Ridge was alleged to be a prominent member of a secret secessionist organization, the "Knights of the Columbia Star," dedicated to resisting "the reelection of Lincoln by all possible means, including force of arms."

This was the Hotspur whom Townsend and Blumenthal arrived to oppose in their Grass Valley *Daily Union*, on airy financial promises from Grass Valley's few staunch Union men.

The first issue of the *Union*, not much larger than a sheet of letter paper, appeared on October 28, 1864, just eleven days before the election. Townsend as editor immediately engaged "Yellow Bird" in an editorial duel, while neighboring Union papers embraced him as a "counteracting influence to the 'moral pestilence' with which Ridge and Byrne have so long poisoned the atmosphere of that locality." With outcries and insults the campaign pitched toward election day. But Jim could not fully give himself to the fight, for he was beset with marital and financial problems. In less than six months his marriage to Elizabeth Lindsey had proved a failure and he and his bride had separated. Furthermore, neither the present nor the future of the *Union* looked at all promising—much of the expected financial support had not come forth, and the paper, having only the political campaign to sustain it, seemed doomed to suspension the day of the election. After all it appeared that Yellow Bird had tangled with a dead duck.

A new hope reared, however, when Ridge buttonholed Townsend and, in behalf of the Copperheads, promised a large sum of money if Townsend and Blumenthal would switch the support of their paper to the McClellan ticket. Jim Townsend heartily approved of the proposition, but his partner, still expecting cash from the Union men, refused the deal and the matter was dropped between them. Ridge later approached Blumenthal in private, allowing him to name his own price if he would reconsider, but Blumenthal replied "that there was not money enough in the town or the State to hire him to do an act so mean and contemptible."

Secretly Townsend and Yellow Bird met once more, deciding to carry off the switch without Blumenthal's knowledge. They agreed that on the following Saturday night the forms for Sunday's edition of the *Union*—the last before the election—would be taken to the *National* office. There the McClellan slate would be substituted for the Union ticket at the head of the editorial column, and an editorial would be added, signed by Townsend, renouncing Unionism and giving support to the Copperheads. The next morning Henry Waite, the carrier for the *Union*, would destroy the regular edition and distribute the bogus one to the subscribers.

Everything went undetected until Saturday evening when Townsend was scheduled to speak at a meeting of the Lincoln and Johnson Club of Grass Valley. When he failed to appear, Blumenthal became suspicious and left the meeting to go directly to the *Union* office. There he confronted the pressman, Sol Shane, who told him of the conspiracy. He then went looking for Jim but found that he had packed all of his belongings and disappeared. With a posse of Union men Blumenthal stood guard at the *Union* office to meet Yellow Bird when he appeared at midnight to take the forms.

Finding that the conspiracy had been discovered, Ridge made no secret of the matter but claimed that the transaction was a "perfectly fair and honorable one." He was allowed to leave without the forms, and the posse stayed to greet Townsend when he arrived about two o'clock—expecting Ridge to return the forms and pay him. Astonished to see the Union posse, Jim at first played innocent but finally confessed—claiming, however, that he had not intended to swindle his partner but would have given him a share of the money. Surprisingly, Townsend too was released—on the condition that he decamp immediately and never appear in Grass Valley again—and that is one promise he did indeed fulfill.

Blumenthal publicized the incident as widely as he could, and Jim Townsend was roundly denounced in the Union press up and down the Mother Lode as an "infamous scoundrel, rascal, dirty scamp and miscreant." Some even demanded that he be hanged from a beam in the printing office. In all this Townsend had underestimated the extent of Union support in Grass Valley, for Blumenthal was not only able to continue the paper but a few months later hired H. C. Bennett, a prominent Mother Lode journalist, as its new editor. The *Union* soon surpassed Ridge's *Nevada National* and it alone is still published today. Ironically, a good bit of the *Union*'s success may well have stemmed from the indignation that Jim's attempted swindle aroused among the

Union men who *then* decided that the paper should not be allowed to fail.

We needn't assess Townsend's behavior in this affair on any profoundly moral grounds. He had gone to Grass Valley to make money. The first betrayal was on the part of the Union men who didn't pay. At the end the only issue Jim apparently saw was whether Blumenthal would have been cheated of his half. Townsend was fundamentally detached, from politics as much as anything else—it is one thing that characterizes his humor. What rankles us perhaps is that it was Honest Abe whom he sold out.

Jim Townsend was drummed out of the Northern Mines, and after failing to get a job in a number of camps, he drifted to Sacramento and then to San Francisco. There in early 1867 he met up once again with Dan Jones and Bill Barnes—back broke from the Comstock. For the next two years they all worked on the radical San Francisco *Daily Times* until October of 1869, when the plant was absorbed into the *Alta California* and Jim with it. Barnes took a job elsewhere in the city, and Jones struck out for Sacramento serving as a hotel steward until he got a case on the *Union*.

But work on San Francisco's morning papers was in no way enviable, for as Jim described it:

The blacksmith, the carpenter, and others, who work in the daytime, can sleep at night, and be refreshed and invigorated; nature not having been overtasked, a pleasant evening has been spent, a good night's rest enjoyed, and a morning consumed in domestic duties, before the labor-hour comes round again. Not so with the printer. He goes to work at ten or eleven o'clock in the forenoon, to 'distribute his cases,' and is perhaps kept dallying about the office waiting for type, 'pasting slips,' and performing other little jobs, until three or four o'clock, when he must go to dinner, and return by six, to go to work again at a time when other men are going home, and to pore over hieroglyphics until broad daylight next morning. After a few hours of restless, unrefreshing sleep, he arises, with a 'big head' and inflamed eyes, to go over the course again in the same manner. Three or four nights are toiled through, and, exhausted physically and mentally, he is compelled to 'put on a sub,' and give nature a chance to recuperate. This is the life of a compositor on a morning newspaper.

Finally in February of 1870, when the Eureka Typographical Union agreed to cut wages from 75¢ to 60¢ a thousand ems, Townsend took his small savings and a likely partner and set out to publish his own newspaper somewhere else. As it turned out, he seems to have settled for anywhere else, for in March he arrived in Antioch.

4

Hog-Reeve

T HE RIVER was smooth and glassy like a mirror; not a breath of air rippled its glittering surface, and, save an occasional sturgeon that leaped from the water, there was nothing to disturb it. The tule-fringed edge of the opposite island was reflected in the river with the vividness of a photograph, seeming to roll and curl away like smoke as the sluggish tide eddied along. Several vessels were becalmed near together, . . . their sails hanging to the mast in sleepy listlessness, as if wearied with waiting for the breeze, while the long streamer at the topmast head of one occasionally fluttered faintly in a vain attempt to display its length. All nature seemed drowsy; even the fish jumped with a lazy tumble, and anglers on the wharves went to sleep while waiting for bites. The sun, too, seemed to be dull, and did not shine with its usual brilliancy, and after feebly struggling all day to pierce the smoky haze which half obscured

it, became tired of shining and went to rest earlier than usual.
Everything was dull and quiet.

THIS WAS the enervated scene that lay before Townsend as he
stepped onto the steamer wharf at Antioch, beside the con-
fluence of the Sacramento and San Joaquin rivers, some forty
miles east of San Francisco. And as he turned to the clustered
houses and stores of Antioch, they imitated that dull and quiet
stretch of water.

But Jim had his customary great hopes for the future of the
town, for its location seemed promising. To the east were miles
of rich bottom lands for farming, and up the canyons to the south
toward Mount Diablo were the coal mines of Nortonville and
Somersville. All the produce from the farms and coal from the
mines fed onto the wharf at Antioch, past which plied each day
at least a dozen steamers for San Francisco, Sacramento, Stock-
ton and other points along the river. The town's listless manner
thus seemed to conceal a vigorous future, one which Townsend
was determined to share.

Jim had chosen as his new partner Henry Waite, his former
carrier and coconspirator on the Grass Valley *Union*. And had
anyone in Antioch been aware of their earlier performance, the
pair might not have enjoyed the hearty reception and cooperation they were given. But in Antioch they were safe from temp-
tation, for there was no one with any loose money to be swindled
out of.

They set up their press and cases in a cramped shed on the
main street, and there on March 26, 1870, they issued the first
number of the weekly Antioch *Ledger*. Their office had no furniture other than the printing equipment and a large dry-goods
box in one corner, which served as the last rest for all unpaid
bills. While Waite was canvassing the merchants for advertising
and setting up the ads, Jim tramped around the town and the
neighboring farms enlisting subscribers and hunting down local
items. Whenever he surprised one of the latter, Townsend would
dash back to his case to lock it safely in type for the coming issue,
for he composed all the material for the paper "on the stick"—
setting it directly in type as the thoughts came to him.

His life was only marginally better than it had been in the city, for each evening after making the "cocktail route" he returned to his rented room to spend a sleepless night—this time listening to stray goats foraging outside the window or, worse yet, desperately fighting off the mosquitoes that shot through the very walls. These pests drove Waite to sell out and seek another climate after only four months—and Jim too was ready to follow when he wrote:

WHO WANTS A MOSQUITO RANCH?

We have traveled some in our day—from the bergs of Greenland to those of the Antarctic, and from the Orient to the Occident. We have battled with the sand-flies of Florida, the gallinippers of Honduras, the horn-bugs of Africa, and the mosquitoes of the Hoogly-Ganges, but we'll be (imagine the expletive) if we ever saw a spot on earth before, where insects were so venomously insulting as they were here on Thursday night. Not a wink of sleep did we get, nor a moment's cessation of scratching, though protected, as we fancied, by a double line of mosquito-bars. We have been told that the oil of penny-royal would knock 'em stiff. We annointed with it, and all night long the volatile stuff made our eyes run water. We rolled hermetically in a sheet, but found a dozen of the pests keeping us company. We got up and donned a gumcoat and long boots, and they punched through these. We lay down with our armor on, and they got under the bed and jabbed up through the mattress. We muffled up in blankets and sat in a chair, thinking we had fooled them then, sure; but with all imaginable ease they would stand on the floor and poke their bills through the bottom of the chair, wounding us in a part we thought most protected. We gave it up—we were skunked; they pegged too many for us, and we arose and went forth, to have a good scratch, and to find some one to hear us swear. We are told by the oldest inhabitant, that in '62 men took their blankets and went to the hills to sleep; and this same old inhabitant says that he don't consider that there are any mosquitoes around while he can see his lights. He's case hardened. If Noah had a male and female mosquito in the Ark with him, and they didn't make him hunt high land in less than forty days, they were not of the same breed we have here.

Editorially Townsend came out foursquare for the public good, sometimes with a hand out for a little cut on the side. When, after commenting for several weeks on all the stray dogs, hogs, cattle and geese—some of them temptingly fat—that roamed about the streets and created a general nuisance, he proposed:

We should revive an old New England custom, and elect a "hog-reeve." Let him come and advertise herein ($2 a square, first insertion), and if the owners are not subscribers to the LEDGER they won't know anything about it, and the hogs will be divided among the poor—that's us and the hog-reeve. We'll be hog-reeve.

But on other occasions his senses demanded relief:

Such a blending of villainous stinks was never suffered before, anywhere, we believe, than in the neighborhood of the Slough. Of itself alone, the puddle can out stink a regiment of skunks but when it is made the receptacle of all the offensive matter collected within a radius of five miles, the stench becomes intolerable. We would like to see the place filled up, but are decidedly opposed to grading it with dead hogs, as is being attempted. A few days ago, somebody, having no fear of the law, nor mercy for the olfactories of half-stifled neighbors, dumped a cart-load of offal into the slough, and before that had "wasted its sweetness" on the air, two defunct porkers were planted there, to rot and fume in the public nostrils; and then, as if this were not carrion enough, Captain Fisher deposited a two hundred pound hog within ten feet of the road. This sort of work should be stopped at once. We will keep a lookout hereafter, and if we see anybody putting offensive skulch there, we'll complain of them in a proper manner. If there is any one who thinks it is not our duty to mention this matter, let him visit the spot and take a good sniff—one will satisfy him.

With the first issue of the *Ledger*, Townsend set a precedent of filling at least one full page with local news each week. This was sheer ambition in a time when most small-town papers were serving up a single column of locals and padding the rest of the paper with patent medicine ads and filler clipped from their city exchanges. It also required a lot of leg work—if not imagination—to round up items. But this policy had immediate rewards in swelling the subscription list, that is, with one exception.

Last week a subscriber to the LEDGER requested us to discontinue sending it to him, giving as a reason that "there is too much local matter in it." Well! We swallow a gallon of wind, and gasp. The idea, "too much local matter." Why if the LEDGER were as large as a ten-acre lot, and issued twice a minute, we would fill it plump full of local matter always, if we could, even though half the items were "steamboats." Our aim, from the beginning, has been to make this paper distinctively local in its character. We didn't intend to meddle in politics, because we are no politician; nor deal in crushing editorials, because the big papers can furnish all the country needs. But we intended it for a home journal—for this country, and no other.

This task became increasingly difficult, however, for it seemed as time went on that local items became harder and harder to find and that the town itself just grew duller and duller.

It was not long before "steamboats" made up the bulk of the locals every week—ranging from a hyperbolic description of a rat fight through colorful vignettes on local citizens to out-and-out tall tales.

A Rat

Anything is good for an item in a country town. Exciting events are so few that the catching of a rat, and his murder by terriers, is of as much interest as a bull-fight elsewhere. Last Saturday morning a huge rat was trapped in one of the stores opposite our office, and brought out into the middle of the street, that all might get a good look at the ferocious animal. A council was held, and a committee appointed to whistle up all the dogs in town. But whistling was unnecessary—there were already several million at hand, each apparently hankering for a bite of rat-meat. The trap-door was opened, and the rodent put out in a lively manner for a crack in the sidewalk; but alas, though "distance lends enchantment to the view," that crack would have been twice as enchanting to the rat had it been ten feet nearer. The dogs were after him, ahead, and over him; a thousand bit him all at once, and each lost his nip, and the rat ran again. The carnage was fearful for a while, until a sprightly little terrier bounded into the canine ring and finished the game with one fell bite.

Townsend's account of single bliss is either hilarious or touching, depending possibly on your own estate.

THE VICISSITUDES OF BACHELOR LIFE

There are few old Californians who have not, at some time, tasted the sweets (in a horn) of bachelor life; when, in the absence of a cook that could make food palatable—and none but a woman can do that for us—he could burn his steak to a crisp and produce a very good imitation of vinegar bitters for his morning coffee. We visited a house last week, where two gentlemen were trying their hand at housekeeping. Two meals had been already cooked by them, and the third was in the process of being spoiled when we entered. What a mess was there, my countrymen! The stock of clean dishes had been exhausted, and each was too lazy to wash them. Upon the table and on the floor lay the debris of previous culinary debauches. Smelling the fumes of something very strange to our olfactories, we inquired the cause, and were told that a Welsh rare-bit was being hatched. We inspected the rare-bit. It was mighty in smell and ponderous in dimensions. Our cookists sought pepper, to add savor to the simmering poultice, called a rare-bit. "Say, Johnny, look up there and see if you can't find some pepper." Johnny seeks and finds, and the seasoning of the mess is perfected. Should any of you desire a recipe for this delicacy, we shall give it. Johnny being assistant cook and ex-officio pot-wallop, was directed by the "chef de cuisine" to prepare the table for the princely repast, which he did, turning the dirty dishes bottom up to get a clean side to eat from; and replenished the table condiments by a fresh supply of mustard, mixed in a blacking box cover. When the table was ready, a dividend was made of what was on the stove, and they sailed in with a vim that induced the belief that they were about to cross the plains, and intended to take aboard a stock sufficient to last them all the way. "Sich is life"—with bachelors.

Occasionally Townsend turned news into narrative, as in this story that rivals that of Saroyan's character who herded cattle on a bicycle in New Jersey.

A STEAM VAQUERO

Last Friday evening, as we were going to press, there was considerable excitement on Galloway's wharf, about a lot of cattle that was being shipped on the steamer Antioch. Some ran overboard, and struck out for Sherman Island. The steamer went in chase, but the animals scattered in all directions, and left "Cap" in a stew about which one to go after. We could see him yanking his bell to "stop her," "turn back," and "go ahead," while Abe was alternating the jingle with, "Spanish steer on the port bow." "Hold on—there's a calf's tail jammed in the wheel-chains!" "Look out, John, or you'll snag her on a bull's horn!" The boat seemed to perspire under the excitement, and several times appeared to be at the point of giving up the chase in disgust. We never saw a steam vaquero before, and don't think the innovation an improvement on the old method of cattle-driving. The animals didn't seem to like the idea of being chased about the river by a bon-fire and did some tall swimming to elude it.

Jim reached down the evolutionary ladder from rats to bugs for this yarn, which he seems to have lifted from *The American Joe Miller* (1865).

A BED-BUG STORY

The other evening, at Frank's, there was a learned dissertation on the subject of bed-bugs and their remarkable tenacity of life. One asserted of his own knowledge that they could be boiled and then come to life. Some had soaked them for hours in turpentine without any fatal consequences. A well-known old codger, who had been listening as an outsider, here gave in his experience in corroboration of the facts. Says he: "Some years ago I took a bed-bug to an iron foundry, and dropped it into a ladle where the melted iron was, and had it run into a skillet. Well, my old woman used that skillet for the next six years, and here the other day she broke it all to smash; and what do you think gentlemen? That er'e insect just walked out of his hole, where he'd been layin' like a frog in a rock, and made tracks for his old roost upstairs. But," added he, by way of parenthesis, "by George, gentlemen, he looked mighty pale."

AFTER Waite sold out in August of 1870, Townsend steered the *Ledger* alone for slightly over four months, until he found a new partner in Joshua P. Abbott. Abbott was two years younger than Jim and also a native of New Hampshire. He had studied law at Dartmouth and had come to California in 1863, only to open an office in Antioch. Slow business had forced him to find a supplementary income, and, since he was unmechanical, he took over most of the editorial and business duties on the paper while Townsend set type and tinkered with the press. This arrangement lasted only three months, until April 5, 1871, when Jim sold out his remaining interest to another printer, Eugene Fuller. Abbott later became sole proprietor, continuing as such for many years.

Leaving Antioch, Townsend went to Sacramento, where he worked for a time on the *Union* with Dan Jones, and then drifted back to San Francisco. Bill Barnes was the first of the three close friends to cross back over the Sierra, returning in 1873, to Nevada, to start a weekly, the *Borax Miner,* at Columbus Salt Marsh near the California line. In five years the camp dwindled to a mere roadside station and Barnes suspended the paper, moving west into California, where Bodie and other camps along the eastern slope of the Sierra were at flood tide. Barnes first settled in the little town of Benton, where he published the *Mono Weekly Messenger* for three months in early 1879 before deciding to move on west to the new camp of Mammoth City, right at the foot of the Sierra. There he founded the *Mammoth City Herald* on July 2, but no sooner had he left Benton than Dan Jones arrived to try his luck.

The mines at Benton had been discovered in 1865 and a town was laid out, but Indian troubles and lack of capital had stifled development, and the town had survived more as a ranching and outfitting center than as a mining camp. The boom of the Bodie mines in the late 1870s brought new notice to the mines of Mono county, and Benton shared in the revival as new companies formed to reopen its long dormant mines. There Dan Jones prepared to re-enter the publishing field, starting one of the most unusual papers ever published in California.

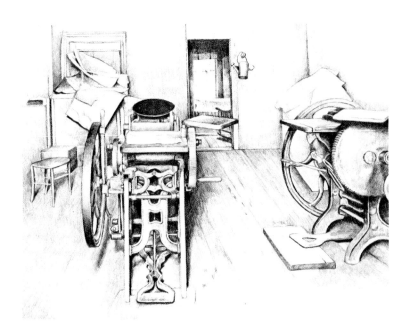

5

The Cheese Press

"**T**HIS PAPER is printed on a cheese press, which for several years did service on the ranch of the Rev. William Harold, down at Bishop Creek," wrote Jones in his salutatory.

The type on which the sheets are worked was assorted from a lot of old printing material which had been purchased by a neighboring mill for use as babbitt metal; the roller which inks the types was prepared by a composition consisting of equal parts of pitch, tar, resin, axle grease, beef tallow, soap and strawberry jam, boiled until of the consistency of india rubber, cast in an oyster can, and then frozen on a lump of Pete Gilhardt's ice; the chase which secures the pages in their position was improvised out of an old and discarded picture frame; the substitutes for column rules, which separate the two columns on each page, were split out of the top of a cigar box; the quoins or wedges, which secure the types in place are pine splinters, and—and yet we are not ashamed of the appearance of the paper today. A machinist is now at work in the office and the press work will be improved with the next issue. Citizens and strangers are invited to inspect the office of the BENTON TRI-WEEKLY LETTER—as illustrating the progress of the arts it is well worth study.

Thus, on the seventh of June, 1879, Dan Jones began the *Tri-Weekly Letter* at Benton. The paper was a tiny sheet with two columns to a page the size of note paper. But despite its size, it thought big. For few printers would have even pretended to turn out a tri-weekly newspaper as a one-man undertaking, and even with help they would never have attempted it in a town so small as Benton. But Dan Jones had a peculiar insanity about such things and leapt into the *Letter* as a one-man show, tri-weekly, in a town of only 150 inhabitants—without even a printing press!

From the very beginning the cheese press was cranky, and it fussed for a full week before it grudgingly issued the second number of the *Letter*. But thereafter the paper truly became tri-weekly. To maintain it, however, Jones worked 14 to 16 hours a day—writing and setting up as much as 40,000 ems a week, in addition to cutting and wetting down the paper, washing and inking the rollers, working the press, and mailing and delivering the paper. Few of the advertisers and subscribers paid in advance—if at all—and he was forced to heat his office on borrowed wood and to get along on one scant meal and a cold lunch per day. Dan summarized his menu as follows: "We have lived on boiled beef with an occasional turnip, and not infrequently on boiled frozen potato and salt for dessert. We would then change our diet to soda crackers and sweetened water for a few days. There is nothing so conductive to health as frequent changes of diet. For the last week or two we have been gourmandizing on bacon and beans straight, with crackers steeped in weak tea. What tobacco we can not beg we buy on credit and we bum our whiskey." Moreover at the end of his long day he had not even a bed or mattress to fall on but was forced to roll up in a couple of blankets and retire on a pile of old exchanges in the corner of the office.

Finally, despite all Dan's efforts, the cheese press collapsed, and for a month no word was heard from Benton. Then on August 14, to the surprise of its former subscribers, the paper was resurrected—to conquer under a new sign, the *Tri-Weekly Bentonian*, on a sheet of manila wrapping paper.

When the cheese press broke down, two of Benton's merchants came to Dan's rescue and fitted up a second makeshift press as a gift. This press was equally unique, having been started a number of years before by some forgotten soul who tried to make an old style copying-press out of wood. About half way through, he had given up in disgust and abandoned the contraption. It was now hauled off the junk heap, refitted with a tympan and blankets, and made to work from an iron screw. And so the one-man press of Dan Jones was under way again.

Even this new adjunct did not reduce the work of getting out the paper, however, and after a few more brief lapses in publication Jones cut the paper to a semiweekly. But even then after six months of publication the paper had averaged only one issue a week—having suspended twice from lack of materials, twice from having completely frozen up in the winter, and a few times from simple intemperance. Moreover, its profits were as irregular as its publication, for of the $456.50 earned by the *Bentonian* during this time, only $56.50 had been paid! Of this sum $21.50 had gone for firewood, $5.50 for freight, $5.00 for rent and washing, and the remaining $24.50 for food. In consequence of such prosperity Dan reduced the paper to a weekly.

Yet despite all such privation Jones managed to keep the few short columns of the *Bentonian* stuffed with lively news items and satirical editorials—many of which were eagerly copied by some of his fatter exchanges. Typical of his editorials was his dissertation on toll roads.

Many years ago in California, when the placer mines began to fail or as was then a popular term, "peter out," the "partners" (always two or more) would be sorely pushed for the means of making grub. (It is always grub in the mountains, hash in the valleys—the terms are synonymous.) In those days the miner's Saturday's clean up would be squandered the following Sabbath day. The firm of a petered placer would shoulder their picks and what little grub they could still run the cheek of the company for at the diggings trading post, and boldly strike out on a prospecting tour. Arriving at some secluded little valley, after a fruitless search for the color, weary, spiritless, and exhausted, they would camp for the night.

Next morning the leader of the party would crawl out of his blanket with a brilliant idea as well as something else in his head. "Boys," he would say, "here is a valley of an acre and a quarter, plenty of wood and an abundance of mountain water—let's open a toll road." He would be laughed at first, but a few explanatory words would soon demonstrate the importance of his proposition. One of the party would be dispatched to the settlements for a whip saw and a printed rate of tolls. The necessary lumber would soon be whipped out and a toll gate erected across the mouth of the canyon gorge. Subsequent mineral discoveries further beyond would necessitate travel on the line of the new toll gate. Pack animals would first find their way up. These would be followed by teams the drivers of which would have to build their road as they went, but they would have to pay toll all the same. A summer's travel with the assistance of the teams and teamster's shovels makes a tolerable toll road.

In a year or so some inquisitive duck begins to question the right of our self-constituted company to collect such enormous tolls. But the sagacity of the ruling spirit is equal to the emergency. He straight-way seeks the necessary quarter to hunt up an imaginary charter. No record of such instrument can be found. There has been carelessness in keeping the books. The Legislature is in session in Sacramento. The (by this time) President of the East South Slide and West Jump Off Turnpike and Toll Road Company, capital stock $500,000, hurries to the capital city, where the judicious use of about as much money as one would expend in having a good time anyhow secures the passage of a bill authorizing Pig Toed Pete, Lop Eared Joe, and One Eyed Bill, and their heirs and assigns, to construct and maintain a toll road between Sure Mire Creek and Bottomless Ravine.

Nine tenths of the toll roads in California have actually been built by those who use them, while others, through bribery and corruption, have been licensed to collect toll on them without the expenditure of a dollar, so to speak.

Dan Jones was also an unrelenting booster whose credo was an absurd faith in the future of the little camp. He proclaimed: "We embarked in this enterprise with implicit faith in the future of this mining region. We believe that we saw what others were too blind or too stupid to see; so, until the grave of Benton is effectually dug, and the body ready to be lowered, *The Bentonian* will continue to be issued every Wednesday morning. And we find that we can do this, too, without either drawing upon our immense mining interest or our large private fortune." But to "parties thinking of visiting our camp in search of employment and having only sufficient coin to pay their expenses to the town," he advised, "send the expense cash by express and stay away. (Cash may be sent in care of the Weekly *Bentonian*.)"

On every available occasion Dan exposed his hearty soul and woeful finances to his subscribers for sympathy and support— but always with a certain salty humor that kept it short of pathos. At the close of his first volume, he summarized the *Bentonian's* plight and that of every other small newspaper venture in the State.

A man considers that when he pays five dollars for a year's subscription he is actually giving the five dollars to help the publisher along. He is doing no such thing. He is simply furnishing the poor devil with just about what it costs him for the raw material with which the paper is manufactured. Take the high price of paper and allow six cents for the white sheet, an additional percentage for the ink, a fraction for the postage, something for the oil to grease the press, a little for wrappers, a trifle for pens and ink, and a slight, a very slight percentage for wasted breath in oaths when some stupid blunder is discovered in the paper or a fellow discovers that a subscriber has sud-

denly got up and dusted and left an unpaid bill, and it can readily be figured out that there is precious little margin left for
profits on newspapers at five dollars a year or twelve and a half
cents a copy.

The BENTONIAN for instance has been the most economically conducted newspaper in America. The publisher has
taken off his coat, and rolled up his sleeves, and performed all
the labor incidental to the printing of the paper. No editors
have been employed, to gossip with visitors and go out and
drink with them. No business men have been engaged to collect bills and spend the money or buck it away at faro. No
printers have found occupation in setting the type, nor boys
kept around to pi it after it was set up. In fact no gentlemen
whatever have been associated with The BENTONIAN during its publication, except our gentlemanly subscribers—and
among whom we are quite proud to class a number of lady
gentlemen.

Economy has been rigidly enforced in every department of
the concern. Not a utensil about it but has been converted to as
many uses as it could possibly be made subservient to. The
large office building with bay windows, of which we have made
frequent mention, is a deserted miner's cabin built of board set
up on end. The great easy chair of which we have so flippantly
spoken is nothing but an old shoe box, with one side stove in,
which we nipped from Creaser & Millner's backyard over a
year ago. The astral lamp which has so long done service in our
midnight studies is nothing but half a potato with a candle stuck
in it. The table on which our ponderous editorials are supposed
to have been written is an old religious Pharoah relic presented
by Dan Ashley, and is now standing in one corner supported by
three legs. The massive silver goblet from which we have so
frequently quaffed the crystal water when athirst, and from
which we have so often sipped our morning coffee, is nothing
but a scoured oyster can, which has served to bear the water for
our domestic use from the Diana mill. The ponderous steam
boiler of which we have frequently boasted is nothing but a
prospector's coffee pot with the spout broken off and two small

holes in the bottom caulked with beeswax forcibly taken from a lady Piute.

Everything else about the "office" is of about the same character. And yet we are frequently asked why do we not go elsewhere where we could rise to a living beyond boiled beef and potatoes. It is true the BENTONIAN man could go to Bodie or some larger town and put his labor in the market, and for which he would receive a weekly stipend. He has gone as long as thirty days in Benton without even feeling a slick quarter. But we have an abiding faith in the future of Benton, and expect to live to hear the screech of the locomotive here and to see bullion shipped away by the ton.

Dan's faith abided him through another six months before the *Bentonian* folded in bankruptcy. During the same time Bill Barnes had ridden the short boom of Mammoth City up to its crest and back down to foreclosure. Thus, hearing of the good fortune of his old friends, Jim Townsend too came over the Sierra to try his luck in Mono.

A decade after he had abandoned Antioch and eighteen years after the Grass Valley scandal, a renewed Jim Townsend with a new, though precarious, reputation arrived in Aurora about May Day, 1880, on a "rantafouzing excursion" among the mining camps with a party of capitalists. He was making a great show at being a mining expert, and the Aurora *Herald* applauded it, billing him as "one of the oldest and best newspaper men on the coast and a miner of no kid-glove experience," who had "wandered over California and Nevada for thirty-one years, during which time he has acted in almost every capacity in connection with mines and mill." He visited a number of the mines around Aurora and uttered glowing and encouraging lies about their value, which the *Herald* quoted as good authority for the imminent prosperity of the camp. Townsend was apparently getting free drinks and an occasional cut from mine owners eager for "expert" praise of their properties and was slowly making the rounds of the mining camps on this income.

After a few weeks in Aurora, Jim was ready to move on before his praise lost its cash value, and he chose as his next stopover the blossoming young camp of Lundy, some thirty miles to the southwest just beyond Mono Lake. Here he was destined to remain for the greater part of two decades.

6

Brass Miners

EONS AGO the deep glacial trough of Lundy canyon was gouged out of the granite and slate fortress that is the eastern slope of the Sierra. The walls of the canyon were polished by the great ice mass as it inched along, and the floor was strewn with the rubble left in retreat. In some places the walls rise nearly vertically to be topped by castellated crags over half a mile above the canyon floor. In other places great talus slides are tearing down the walls rock by rock to a more gradual repose. The floor of the canyon, eight thousand feet above the sea, is crowded with dense groves of aspen and Jeffery pine and thickets of snow bush, bitter brush, and berries. At its upper end, Mill Creek enters the gorge over a five hundred foot fall, which forms a sparkling ribbon from early spring to midwinter, when it crystallizes to a great icicle. The creek meanders slowly down among the groves, ponds, and thickets to Lundy Lake, a long, serene body of water lying restrained behind a glacial moraine half way down the canyon. Leaving Lundy Lake the creek cuts a narrow course through the glacial debris and cataracts out of the canyon into the broad saline basin of Mono Lake. There is no more idyllic canyon to be found anywhere along the great range.

Late in the fall of 1879, rich silver lodes were discovered high on the slopes of Lundy Canyon, and with the coming of spring the following year the rush to the new mines began. Early in April, prospectors began work in the canyon, and by the first of May carpenters were hammering in the meadow above the lake. Within a month the feverish activity erected more than thirty buildings on the meadow, and the town of Lundy materialized.

When Townsend arrived in June 1880, the new town was ready to chase its seven saloons with a weekly newspaper, the *Homer Mining Index*. Its office was a shed, located at the junction of two freshly cleared trails, known on the town plat as Second and B streets. The furnishings of the office were much akin to those of Dan Jones' *Bentonian* with the exception of a new printing press and type just shipped from San Francisco. There Jim found Joe Baker and John Curry in shirt sleeves preparing the first number of their paper to be issued the following Saturday. Townsend and Baker, the future editor, hit it off well, and Jim hung around the office for some time spinning yarns and throwing his moral, if not physical, back into the venture.

On June 12, in the paper's first issue, Baker announced Jim's advent to the community.

All sorts of odd characters are constantly turning up, like unexpected barrel hoops, in a place like this. The other day the editorial staff of THE MINING INDEX stumped the toe of his recollection against Jim Townsend (old Jim), one of the oldest printers on the Pacific Coast, who has stuck type and wielded a lead bludgeon in half the newspaper offices this side of the "Big Rockies." A queer old stick is Jim with as many kinks in his mental make-up as a piece of mountain mahogany, and as jolly a dog as ever "proved a galley." "A fellow of infinite jest" is this stray old print—one of your good Western talkers—whose stories combine the flavor of the mining camp and the *bonhomie* of the Bohemian over his beer. He is prospecting in Homer District, thinking there is more money in it than in the manufacture (in his mind) of "flying machines" in Sacramento. All his old friends of the craft will wish Jim more success in this venture than he met with in his aerial navigation experiments.

The following week, while Baker was busy composing heavy editorials deploring the camp's lawlessness—two unpunished murders and three shooting affrays in four weeks—and reprimanding the camp's do-nothing claim holders for "doing the wall-flower business in the saloons, and lying around in penniless expectancy," Townsend dropped back into the office to give Curry a hand by fattening up the local columns with some of his own creations. He opened with a graphic description of the locale:

The country about us is the roughest under the sun. There is no region to which we can compare it. The roughest neighborhood of Virginia City is a race-track in comparison. The hills surrounding us rise to an altitude of 2,000 feet above the town, and in many places their sides are perpendicular for several hundred feet, and in not a few instances the summit projects beyond the base. There is no mountain about here so sloping that a man can climb straight up its side. To scale the easiest of them a prospector needs claws like a jaybird and a grip like a nut-cracker. A view of Lundy Canyon from the summit at its head suggests that the Creator made a great chasm by splitting a mountain in twain, and then turned it inside out, like a sock. The atmosphere is so clear that one is woefully deceived in distances. You start to climb a hill that looks like a modest knoll, and after two or three hours' desperate struggling you are tempted to swear that the hill grows faster than you can climb, and that its top is crawling away from you. But this is the place for tunnels and dumps. If the Sutro tunnel had been run into one of these hills it would not now have a dump big enough to land a wheelbarrow on.

And to fill out the column he threw in a little patter on its growth, revealing his democratic social attitudes as well.

Prospectors, visitors, mining experts and capitalists are pouring in upon us like a snow-slide. There is a continuous procession of buggies, wagons, horsemen, pack-mules and pedestrians coming up the canyon, and every secluded nook and dell adjacent to the creek is a camping-place of new arrivals. A man with a "biled" shirt on is set down as a bloated capitalist from Bodie, and an "expert" is readily known by his brassy stare and general aspect of imbecility. Lundy in the evening looks like the camping-ground of an army. Fires twinkle and glimmer among the grand old pines while the weary prospector wrestles with gutta-percha hog-meat and windy beans, or deftly flips the toothsome slapjack. Tents and brush shelters signify that their occupants have been delicately reared; the middle class bivouac on the lee side of a log, while the real hearty old mountaineer curls himself up on a granite shelf and snores the bullfrogs out of countenance. Nights are just cool enough to render a pair of blankets necessary, so that sleeping in the open air is no hardship. Without fear of contradiction we assert that the climate of Lundy at this season of the year is incomparable. But it's a holy terror in Winter, we should remark.

Townsend continued to help out on the paper for the next two weeks, peppering the local column with a variety of quips. It was for such epigrams as these that he was to be best known during the following decade when the papers of Nevada and the Mother Lode copied them religiously each week under the simple heading of "Townsendisms."

Mill Creek is so crooked in one place that it is difficult to cross it. We waded it half a dozen times the other day and came out on the same side every time.

The waters of Mono Lake are so buoyant that the bottom has to be bolted down, and boys paddle about on granite boulders.

Wild onions are plentiful hereabouts, and the eaters thereof smell like the back door of a puppy's nest.

"When thieves fall out honest men get their dues." But when honest men fall out lawyers get their fees.

The editor of the PIOCHE RECORD says, "Mrs. Page's milk is delicious." We shall soon hear that her husband has weaned him with a club. He knows too much.

Aurora, Nevada, wants a church. We are willing to risk our hopes of salvation on a quartz mill. There is more civilization in the thump of one stamp than in a hundred sermons.

And to further fatten up the pages he contributed a few vignettes on the local scene. We believe that such writing from this period shows a quantum leap in his narrative skill.

A Social Cloudburst

An unexpected event last Sunday gave Lundy folks such a start that none of them have thought to kill a man since. A party of ladies and gentlemen from Bodie broke in upon the usual Sunday spree in all the glory of straw hats, linen ulsters and other picnic apparel, causing the miners to stare, the dogs to bark and the logging cattle to low in sheer amazement. Even "Butch's" black pig gave a grunt of astonishment. The feminine invasion caused a great commotion among the old prospectors, who immediately inaugurated a run on Rosenwald, Coblentz & Co.'s store for calico shirts and bandana handkerchiefs. There was an active demand for blacking, and one old "shellback" was in such a hurry to get spruced up that he gave a man an interest in a million-dollar claim to spit for him while he polished his boots. The barber, who has been holding down the cushions of his chair in idleness for the past two months, was overwhelmed with customers. All wanted to be shaved "right away," and pistols were drawn several times to settle disputes about who was next. But a saloon-keeper from "Frisco" took the shine out of the whole lot by appearing gorgeously arrayed in a plug hat, "biled" shirt, barber-pole socks, and a vest with a whole flower-garden on it. Fifty men agreed that he looked like a darned monkey, and swore unanimously that he kept the worst whisky in town—a fact that they had not previously discovered. Talk about the civilizing effect of a church! Fifty good-looking girls will do more civilizing in a mining camp than all the preachers in Christendom.

Here Townsend turns his discerning vision again on bugs, and almost manages to tell the truth.

The Sly Woodtick

Of all the myriad of bugs which our ingenious Lord has invented to pester us, the Mill Creek woodtick is boss. The thing is about the size of a lodging-house bed-bug, which it no more resembles than a Lundy nabob resembles a Bodie bummer. It has a shell like a terrapin, with mouths all around, and a dozen or two of legs, each one armed with a diamond drill. It burrows in the flesh like a gopher, and often becomes distended with blood to the size of a hazel nut, when it drops off leaving an egg in the cavity. This germ causes an intolerable itching and burning, and a sore that is sometimes difficult to heal. It is next to impossible to guard against them. Men are attacked in the most sensitive places, and out of a dozen persons sitting in a saloon or anywhere else about three or four will all the time be popping up as if hoisted out of a pigeon-trap, shrieking "Goddlemity!" The newcomer is startled and inquires the cause of this queerness. The reply is: "Woodticks. Carpet tacks and patent rat-traps ain't nothin' to 'em."

Finally, Townsend found the celebration of an unglorious Fourth of July in these mountains a topic well worth deadpanning.

On account of several unforeseen accidents the programme for our Fourth of July celebration will have to be altered in several particulars. Mr. Coblentz being sick, Dutch Harry will fill the post of honor as Orator: Jim McLaughlin will personate the Goddess of Liberty, and in the absence of a flag will carry aloft a broom. As Maestretti's English is a little broken, it has been decided for him to whistle his poem. The steamboat having failed to arrive, the excursion will be limited to a bonfire on the bank and a wade in the shallow water. The fiddle which was to have supplied the music at the ball was wrecked coming from Bodie by a passenger using it for a cushion; therefore we cannot have a dance as advertised. Instead there will be a grand sweepstake dogfight, free for all and catch weight, at which there will be free whiskey to keep the fires of patriotism from flagging. Arrangements have been made to secure fine weather, and a few rough-and-tumble fights will be sandwiched in between the other ceremonies to prevent any appearance of monotony.

By the end of its fourth week the paper was well established and on fairly sound footing financially, but not so sound that its proprietors could afford to pay an extra printer any more than a thank you and an occasional drink. Therefore, Townsend set out to con his fortune in the surrounding mines. His first scheme was to try to promote a powerful pumping machine on the shore of Mono Lake to send lake water some ten miles to the Bodie mines for amalgamating ore. He loudly contended that the waters of the lake contained just the right amount of soda, borax and salt to "work the most rebellious ores up to 110 in the shade," and that the local mining experts were asses not to have thought of it before. But the miners remained asses, and Jim next took a lease on an arrastra in the old Mono diggings at the foot of Lundy Canyon near the Mono Lake shore. He ran the arrastra for ten days, crushing ore from a couple of the mines at Lundy at a healthy profit of $40 a ton.

His success convinced Townsend that he should build an arrastra of his own nearer the source of the ore in Lake Canyon, main tributary to Lundy Canyon, which it enters right above the townsite. He constructed a small model and caught the stage to Aurora, where he hoped to get financial backing. After an unsuccessful tour of Aurora's saloons, buying a drink for every man who would listen to his new scheme, Jim dropped into the *Herald* office to put in another plug for his arrastra, which, after all the retelling, was already in the course of construction. Mack Glenn, the editor, gave him a sympathetic ear, but no money, even though Townsend was certain that the venture could not help but succeed in a district where "the gold sticks out of the quartz in chunks as big as the HERALD office, and actually begs for quicksilver." Those with money were not so certain, however, and after a week of fruitless promoting Jim returned to Lundy. Here, lacking the money to build an arrastra for himself, he contracted to build one for two Lake Canyon mine owners, Andy Howk and Abner Travis.

Townsend hired four men and started work in mid-September, completing the arrastra in the first week of October. It was a large affair—with a crushing area fifteen feet in diameter and a drag driven by a nine-foot hurdy-gurdy wheel—capable of crushing two tons of ore a day. Jim said modestly that it was the best and most complete arrastra in the country, and Joe Baker of the

Mining Index agreed that it was indeed "constructed on the most scientific method, illustrating Jim's aptitude for mechanics, which is only excelled by his capacity for whisky, which is simply unlimited."

With Townsend as chief engineer the arrastra began crushing ore in early October and ran for six weeks before the approach of winter froze the flume and the whole operation.

The fortunes of the *Homer Mining Index* had not panned out nearly as rich as its founders had anticipated, and in less than two months John Curry sold out his share of the paper to his partner, Joe Baker. Curry also fancied himself to be a mining expert, a far better one than a printer or publisher. So immediately after quitting the paper, he took off with another partner on a prospecting expedition to Leevining Creek, half a dozen miles south of Lundy. The trek dragged out for several weeks, and the partners consumed a mountain of provisions, but all for no reward. As Townsend later described it, the adventure added not a tittle to Curry's stature as a mining expert.

CURRY'S BRASS MINE

Some months ago Bob Cameron and John J. Curry came into camp from a prospecting trip, looking very owlish, and exhibiting samples of rock from a tremendous vein they had discovered. Assays subsequently showed a value of several cents a ton. From the appearance of the samples it was suspected at the time that the boys had located the levee at the north end of Oneida Lake; but we now know that they had actually found something, and are not surprised that they should wear a puzzled and mystified look. Other parties have since jumped the claim and extracted a large amount of ore which, if it be anything at all, is nearly pure brass. The metal has been tested in various ways, both here and in Bodie, and the result is the same: brass. It is proposed to form a company to work this metallurgical monstrosity, and to manufacture its product into merchantable articles. One of the parties concerned remarked to the INDEX man: "We've got stuff enough in sight to fence in the whole d——d country with brass candlesticks ten feet high." The original discoverers have no doubt missed a good thing. We asked Bob why he didn't stay and try to do something with his discovery. Then his nose twinkled and his eyes got green. Said he: "You don't know what I suffered on that trip. Every night, after we'd got tucked away under the blankets, Curry'd begin, 'When I was State Printer in Oregon —,' and I'd have to climb a tree to escape his infernal ding-dong about what a big man he used to be in Oregon. You know, he had a way of nudging a fellow at every word or two. Well one day I was leaning against a big tamarack, and he came up and started on his old rigmarole. I just slipped down and crawled away, and left him to bore that tree as much as he liked. When I got back to camp, six or seven hours afterward, dern my skin if he hadn't nudged that tamarack clean off and started in on an oak stump. Oh, I couldn't stand it and had to come home."

Baker in the meantime had been struggling single-handed to keep the paper going, and his being a slow typeslinger didn't help. Thus when the first freeze shut down Jim Townsend's arrastra, Baker was pleased to offer him a job for the winter months, or even better, the whole paper at a fair price. Townsend agreed to work on the paper until the first of the year with the option to buy at that time, presumably with whatever wages he had earned going toward the purchase price. Just before Thanksgiving Jim took the case of the *Mining Index* to flood its readers in a renewed torrent of humorous quips and local items. He first burlesqued the sad plight of an unfortunate visitor who had become the goat for a prank of the local bummers.

A Mill Creek "Goat"

A Frenchwoman of doubtful reputation, or rather not at all doubtful, came over here from Bodie, a few days ago. She was not fair, but she was fat and probably forty. She was accompanied by a black and tan terrier of diminutive size on which she lavished a wealth of affection. The morning after her arrival she sauntered out to see the town with the dog for an escort. She had not been out more than half an hour before "Billy" was missed. After calling and searching for him frantically, she gave way to tears, and said she would give ten dollars to anyone who would return the dog. "Billy" had been packed off in the overcoat pocket of one of the "b'hoys." She was told that the dog would be returned if she would pay the ten dollars and she readily assented to the bargain. But when the dog was produced, she said she had no money. The finder of the dog refused to give him up, and drawing a huge cheese-knife swore that his head, like Buckingham's, should roll from his body if the ten dollars was not immediately forthcoming. She wept hysterically on receiving this ultimatum, and begged piteously for the life of her dog, but the obdurate wretch savagely declared that he should proceed with the execution if he did not get the money in half an hour. The poor creature rustled around and borrowed the money for "Billy's" ransom. When she had him once more in her arms, she cried, laughed and kissed him all in one breath, and talked to him, amid her sobs, affectionately in French. The boys laughed themselves dry at the scene, and then went into a saloon and spent the ten dollars for whisky.

But occasionally even the pranksters got hoisted on their own jokes, as Townsend was happy to record in "The Tables Turned":

It has been a favorite joke of the officers here to get some man to try on the handcuffs, and then "soak" the key to some saloon keeper for the drinks. The victim of misplaced confidence would have to redeem the key to get released. A few days ago one of the officers got badly left on a joke of this kind. Jim Slack, Deputy Constable, got Charley Hector to try on the "bracelets," just for fun. When they were securely fastened, Jim soaked the key at the Snowflake Saloon for a dollar's worth of whisky. Charley refused to put up, and after a while Jim took a walk, leaving his victim to meditate on the pleasures of being handcuffed. While Jim was absent Charley redeemed the key, and then pawned the handcuffs for eight dollars' worth of whisky. When Jim returned he gave in that he was beat, set up the whisky and redeemed his jewelry.

Townsend was also semiconscious of his civic duty and warned his fellow Lundyites of a new menace to their health and safety:

"New barber in town! He is a boss man at skinning. Served his time in a slaughter-house. All his patients wear a sticking-plaster mask. Kill him!" And in support of the invective he offered the gruesome details.

The man who submits his face to the manipulations of an itinerant latherer takes many chances. One of those soap-pot butchers entered Kirkpatrick & Norton's store the other day and offered to shave the crowd. Norton, who has a beard like a wool-carder, availed himself of the offer and submitted to the preliminaries of an operation. The artist laid out his meat-saws and scalpers. At the first stroke he handsomely missed the old man's jugular and made a saw-notch in his off ear. The blood flew. The soap-fiend was delighted, and made a dash for his victim's chin, with still greater success. The subject's shirt-front by this time resembled the Dutch flag in distress, and a suspension of hostilities was called for by the bystanders. The barber inquired: "Does it go easy?" "Well, that depends," replied the bleeding victim. "If you call this operation skinning, its not so bad; but if you're trying to shave me, I don't want any more of it." And the artist sought other faces to gash.

But graver problems were soon to beset the fledgling camp, for winter was coming fast upon Lundy.

7

Toe Jam and Bull Butter

THE COMING of winter in Lundy Canyon is an awesome and sometimes terrifying event as Townsend was later to learn. By mid-fall the numbing cold has reached down from the ice-bound crags of the summit, down the ravines and gorges into Lundy Canyon, nipping the last leaves from the aspen. Then slowly the wind begins to rise—just a soft breeze in the first weeks, its crescendo quickly mounting until at last it bursts down the canyon with a frightening blast, unleashing an avalanche of new snow to cover its wake of havoc.

Of his first encounter with the Lundy zephyrs Jim wrote:

The wind here is a holy terror to people who were raised in a dead calm. A puff will turn a dog inside out, and several stage companies have been busted by trying to keep paint on their wagons. I lived in a solid log cabin built against a granite ledge, and yet the wind is so strong that our habitation danced a jig every time a gust came down the canyon, and now we have been blown across several lots, and our house threatens to trot down into the lake. A man who comes here wants a claw like a jaybird and about 100 pounds of old iron in the seat of his breeches, else he leaves camp schooner rigged.

Shortly he had an even wilder sample when Lundy's newest hotel died an early death.

About 7 o'clock a fierce gust came down Main street, and, taking the new hotel "broadside on," slid it from its underpinning and deposited it in the adjoining lot, leaving a double twist in the structure which could make a blind man cross-eyed to contemplate. All the dishes, bar fixtures and lamps in the house were smashed to atoms, and the interior wrecked beyond repair. The whole was demolished and now lies in a confused heap, like a junk-shop with a severe attack of colic. A considerable portion of the material broke through the floor and dropped into a well beneath. Had an earthquake occurred in the house the wreck could not have been more complete.

But then the snow came, falling to depths of many feet on the flats and blown by the wind into six-foot drifts in the street and completely choking off the road down the canyon. So rapid was the onset of the storm that many unwary prospectors were trapped at their claims high on the slopes and were badly frozen and frostbitten before they could reach shelter—sometimes less than a mile away. All contact with the outside world was cut off, and as the days passed, a new calamity descended upon the camp: the supply of whisky was rapidly being consumed. Townsend sensed the impending terror and warned, "Great distress is imminent in Lundy. Half the saloons are out of whisky, and the stock in others is very low. If there is not a hegira soon there will be a whisky famine." But the snowdrifts held and the calamity came—the last drink of whisky was gone!

For three days there was great trouble and tribulation among the old soakers, and many a countenance was bleached by enforced temperance into an expression of stolid solemnity. Many new-fangled substitutes for the real stuff were devised. Col. Kikendale got up one that had quite a run. In fact, the boys stuck to it till the stock of ingredients gave out. It was compounded of hot drops, red pepper and absinthe, and went down one's throat like a disbanded torch-light procession. It was called the "Wake up Jake," and was very popular. Bronson got up a drink which he designated the "Toe Jam." It was composed of jinger tea, pepper-sauce and jalap, and those who partook of it were considerably stirred up inwardly. Haas concocted a beverage which became known as the "Holy Terror." It was made of sheep-wash, vinegar and potash. This was immensely popular, as it was like unto a gargle of cross-cut saws. When these fancy drinks were exhausted the boys were disconsolate, and moped about like distempered pups till the camp was electrified by the news, "Barrel o' whisky down below the lake!" Then every man begged, borrowed or stole a long-handled shovel, and valiantly marched to the rescue of that whisky barrel. Corporal Collamer was there, and by his indefatigable endeavors gained the title of "The Great American Snow-drift Annihilator." The boys were terribly afraid that the whisky would freeze before it could be got under cover. But it is safe now, and is being rapidly dispensed to the thirsty crowd. Next week we will have about nineteen fights to record.

True to prediction the whisky was intemperately downed while the saloon-keepers once again drove away the bummers. "Passing the Snowflake Saloon last night we heard the Colonel or his bar-creature ejaculating: 'Now get out o' here, you damned-drunkensyphiliticstiffs! Swim clear o' this caravansary, you pestilent calamities! If any of you rusty old bums starts a song he'll die instanter. Hand me that gun.'"

Jim was pleased to observe, however, that the whisky famine did have one good effect upon the camp. "During the past week probably one hundred men have left the camp for other parts, some with the intention of returning in early spring, others with no intention at all. It is well for the town to be rid of the drones. The whisky famine was very hard upon them. They could sleep in the brush and live without grub but when it came down to compulsory total abstinence they lit out for Bodie."

Among those that lit out for Bodie was Joe Baker who had gone to draw up the final papers for the sale of the *Index*, and, more important, to locate a partner for Townsend, who had found he could afford only half of the establishment. During Baker's absence Jim's first try at going it alone forced him the following week to confess:

The INDEX wears a cadaverous aspect this week. It is the un-avoidable result of a concatenation of congruous circumstances. The boss has gone to Bodie on special business. The devil has been taking medicine, so that his work at the "case" has been spasmodic and jerky. The printing office is open on all sides, and the snow flies in where it pleases. In the morning every-thing is frozen solid. Then we thaw things out, and the whole concern is deluged with drippings. It is hard to set type under such conditions. When the office is dry it is too cold to work in; when it is warm the printer needs gum-boots and oil-skins. In fact, it has been a hell of a job to get this paper out.

Despite Townsend's ill-timed display of honesty, Baker suc-ceeded in unloading the other half of the *Index* on a former Vir-ginia City printer, Ed Everett. They both returned to Lundy, and on January 1, 1881, the paper changed hands. Townsend and Everett were quick to make plain their intentions to the people of Lundy, announcing: "We have taken hold of THE INDEX for the purpose of making a living. We are not here for our health. We expect that every man who makes his living in this district will assist this paper to some extent. If we labor to help the camp, we shall expect the people of the camp to help us!"

And thus they stepped bravely into the new year optimistic that the camp would have a population of 10,000 by summer. Townsend said, in fact, a company had been organized to set the mountains back to widen the townsite. But winter was still tight-ening its grip on the camp and summer's beckoning prosperity was a long way off. So for the time, Jim found solace in hot Tom-and-Jerrys at the Snowflake and the O. K. Sample Room and made do with such culinary rarities as bull butter. The drink provided "a world of spiritual comfort" but the latter, though having a not disagreeable flavor when first broached, in three days acquired the distinctive taste of "salve that has done duty upon a sore heel." With such a choice, Jim stuck to Tom-and-Jerrys, the better to aid the creation of good news items.

But Townsend's most consistent source of entertainment that winter was to be found in the proceedings of Judge Medlicott's justice court. Here Jim crowed and clucked as he made comic opera of Lundy's judiciary, writing, during the ensuing weeks, of things unprecedented in uncommon law.

Lundy's court occupied the front room of a lodging house and its walls were decorated with large charcoal sketches of local notables. In the most prominent position was a caricature of the Judge himself, of which Jim wrote that "the sketcher shows his wonderful skill in nasal architecture, and builds a proboscis which is readily recognized. It looks something like a cross between a step-ladder and the scoop of a steam-paddy. A syringe is being applied to the starboard orifice of this monstrous nose, and somebody in the background is apparently working it for the purpose of sluicing out his Honor's head—a negative hint that the fountain of justice should be clear."

Immediately beside this was a rendering of Colonel Kikendale, the Deputy District Attorney and proprietor of the Snowflake Saloon, whose portrait, according to Jim, looked "like a horse's foot in a sock, and yet the Colonel's features are there complete, all except the ears—there is not room for them unless the roof is raised. They will probably be finished when the weather will allow the artist to work out-doors. The Colonel is pictured with a bottle in one hand and a cinch in the other, which, perhaps, signifies that the contents of the former give him strength to apply the latter to evil-doers." And nearby was a sketch of Deacon Parkinson, the aged, part-time editor of the Carson *Tribune*, who was wintering in the wilds of Lundy and occasionally acted in behalf of the defense. This sketch showed "a patriarchial face, with a mixed expression of hope and repentance. The coloring of the nose is perfect, and the peak has its natural drop, while the left eye is cocked upon the Colonel with a quizzical leer, as if the Deacon were saying: 'This is the way I long have sought, old pard. It don't make any difference which sides we're on, one of us is bound to win, unless they turn this shebang into a court of equity and fire us both out.'"

Other panels depicted the postmaster, the constable, a local tough, and sundry characters including the "Mill Creek Editor." Jim was quite fond of his portrait although he felt moved to explain that "his head is lop-sided with the weight of a big quill, with which he has apparently been making out bills, and the expression denotes an intense desire that the many who are indebted to THE INDEX should come forward and pungle." A final frame vividly portrayed the local jury reaching a verdict, wherein two jurors who had declined to agree were "having the stuffing jumped out of them by the other ten, who hear the glasses jingle on the adjacent bar, and are anxious to get out, for they realize that the party winning the case will 'set 'em up lively.'" Jim opened his court proceedings with

A REMARKABLE CASE

One of the greatest trials in the criminal annals of Mill Creek came off a few days since before Judge Medlicott. The defendant was a Chinese vegetable peddler. The complaint charged him with horse stealing. Col. Kikendale appeared for the outraged and indignant people. Judge Parkinson was retained for the defense. As he was a little rusty in his law, he thought he would consult some authorities. He hunted all over town for law books and finally succeeded in finding several Patent Office Reports and a copy of Copp's Mining Laws. Armed with these he entered the court-room and announced himself ready for trial. There ensued such a forensic duel as would have made Rome howl, even in the days of Cicero. The fortunes of the legal battle fluctuated many times during the exciting contest. At first it appeared that Col. Kikendale would be convicted, but he succeeded in turning the enemy's flank, and then it seemed as if the crime would be fastened on Deacon Parkinson. However, the Deacon established an alibi by a witness who testified that the Deacon was taking a drink with him at the time of the alleged stealing. As the fray went on Judge Medlicott became in imminent peril of being brought in as the true culprit, but he proved that at the time of the robbery he was walking toward Wasson with a package of candy in his left breast pocket, and thus cleared his skirts and eased the minds of all the young ladies in the neighborhood. Finally they got around to the poor old Chinaman, and fastened all sorts of high crimes and misdemeanors upon him. He could not repel the charges because he could speak no English. It was proved that the Chinaman took a horse belonging to a man here in town, without leave, and went down to Mono Lake for a load of vegetables. When this daring old rheumatic thief returned with the horse and his truck, the argus-eyed and vigilant minions of the law pounced upon him. As a proof of his total depravity and felonious disposition, it was cited that he had the unexampled hardihood to bring the horse right back here, where he and the horse were known to everybody. This was convincing and the reckless old villain was convicted of horse stealing. Then justice pronounced her dreaded fiat—fined the Mongolian purloiner of horse-flesh forty dollars. Thus ended a case of great legal and political significance. The principle that our liberties must be preserved from the insidious Chinese was fully and triumphantly vindicated.

Not to get solemn about it, but such humanity-through-irony as Jim displays here was becoming increasingly risky in the racist atmosphere leading to the Chinese Exclusion Act of 1882.

This litigation was followed a few weeks later by "An Absorbing Trespass Case."

On Tuesday Henry Klein and Ed Costello were arrested for "malicious trespass" upon the mining ground claimed by Mrs. Clara Moss, "the female prospector." The Justice at first refused to issue a warrant, believing that the result would be but the saddling of useless expense upon the county. The Deputy District Attorney, however, made a preemptory demand for the warrant and it was issued. A jury trial was demanded and the district was ransacked for jurors. Had the lives of the arrested men been at stake, there could have been no more difficulty in obtaining twelve jurymen than was experienced in this simple case of alleged trespass. The trial began in Judge Medlicott's court-room, and that not having sufficient capacity to hold the curious crowd, the court adjourned to the Snowflake Saloon. Here the sublime proceedings continued. Klein was attorney for the defense, and Kikendale and Parkinson invoked the wrath of the outraged people of the State of California. There was music in the air from the start. At times everything seemed to be in an inextricable snarl, and spectators momentarily expected to see attorneys, witnesses, and jurymen rise in a body and open a fusilade on the Judge, who barricaded himself behind a row of whisky barrels and piled on fines for contempt three tiers deep. After a long but not tedious trial the case was submitted to the jury, who were locked up in the saloon to deliberate, while the crowd paddled around town in the snow and slush, to await the verdict. About three o'clock this morning the Judge became impatient and peeked in at the window to see how they were getting on. They were progressing finely. They were seated at the table drinking the Colonel's whisky, and apparently playing "freezeout" for the verdict. This sort of trifling was stopped and shortly after they announced that they had agreed to differ. They stood "six and six." It was the Judge's deal, and he dismissed the case. When the prosecuting attorney was wanted, he came into the court in slippers, closely buttoned up in a lady's ulster and his hair sticking up as if he had received an invitation to Jack Hall's ghost party. His peculiar rig caused much speculation. Were it not for the well known rigid morality of the Colonel, evilminded persons might be disposed to smell a mice.

And the whole proceedings were soon reduced to dramatized farce under the pro-tempore guidance of assayer Wilcox.

An Interesting Trial

On Wednesday evening one of the most interesting trials that the history of Mono county tells of took place at Wilson's Wine

Rooms in this town. It was the case of the State versus one T——, and the charge was an attempt at stealing a kiss from a high-toned female on the Main street of Lundy, and in open daylight. The gay young Lothario defended his own case with the assistance of another young aspirant for legal honors. The jurors were Ass. Campbell, Bob Peterson, Clark Barney, Drake Francis, Voorhees Van and Putnam George, all of the town of Bodie. Judge Wilcox occupied the apex of a gin barrel, and the District Attorney sat on a coal oil can at the judicial feet. Seventeen special constables were appointed by his honor for the purpose of keeping the stiffs in order. The Judge called the Court to order in the following words: "You d——d loafers, Mill Creek bummers and Bodie frauds, this is a Court of Justice, and by the holy Moses I'll let you know that you hain't got no dam slouch for a squire this time. The first fellow that chips I'll fine twenty-five drinks." On the District Attorney rising to a question of privilege, his honor hit him a lick on his smooth top and inquired if the damphool imagined himself in the Legislative halls. "No one but myself and the defendant has any privilege in this 'ere Court, and don't you forget it."

(It may be mentioned here that the reason the jury was selected from the Bodie loafers was that none of the Mill Creek men pay taxes.)

The following oath was then put to the jurors and attending witnesses, to which all subscribed: "You and each of you solemnly swear that to the best of your knowledge and belief you never did and never will tell the truth in this case or any other, so help you Judas Iscariot."

The jurors, before being accepted, were submitted to the following rigid examination:

First juror—Do you know anything? A.—No. Q.—Did you ever commit a crime? A.—No. Q.—Did you ever do a good act? A.—Only once, and then I fainted. Passed.

Second juror—Have you any conscientious scruples in the matter of the death punishments or any other? A.—No. By defense—Have you scruples of any kind? A.—No, only a few grains. Passed.

Third juror—Do you know anything of the defendant in this

case? A.—Yes, I have seen him not only pursue but hug a squaw in the neighborhood of the printing office. By defense— Did you consider that there was any offense in that? A.—Yes. "Then you are a durned fool, and unfit to sit anywhere." At this stage of the proceedings the juror capsized the bench, threw a lamp at the attorney, spit out his "chaw" into the judge's mouth, piled the remaining jurors in a heap, and grabbing the complaining witness around her voluminous waist made tracks for the open air and disappeared. The Judge pitched into the District Attorney, and the defendant, who had been busy abstracting whisky-bottles from the coat pockets of the jurors, jumped the table of justice, and in a stentorian, sailor-like voice shouted, "All hands to grog! Beat 'em by the holy poker!"

THE NEW year also brought the annual swearing-off time— the strength of the resolutions varying, with that of the resolvers, from total abstinence to red-nosed temperance. Townsend would have none of it, but delighted in the attempts of others who sometimes found the cure much worse than the affliction.

Two prominent Lundy business men of the tender age of 55 years made a mutual agreement to quit the filthy habit of smoking and chewing tobacco. There was no money bet nor any written agreement entered into concerning the infraction of the bargain; but only the word of honor passed between the two gentlemen. On Tuesday one of the ex-tobacco men jammed his protuberant nose against a barrel of sugar while rolling it into his store; kicked the constable out of the building for summoning him on a jury; killed a little pet dog for licking the sore proboscis, and stole money from his own pants pockets. On Wednesday the other party to the anti-tobacco contract went to the saw mill early in the morning and because the saw did not run as smoothly as usual beat the teeth of the main saw, smashed the top saw, threw the engineer into the furnace, and set fire to a pile of dry lumber prepared for the building intended for his family residence. On Thursday morning a mutual friend was called into council and after a deal of squirming the affair was settled, but not until the employees of the saw mill had, in a body, demanded their pay and discharge. If ever real fun was had in such a peculiar mining camp as Lundy, it was when the two semi-centarians shook hands, and, rubbing noses, blew the smoke of their cigars in each other's faces. Everybody was happy and peace prevails at the mill and the store.

All resolutions seem made to be broken, and even so moderate a movement as Judge Medlicott's Dusenberry Reform Club, with its stringent motto "never drink more than you can hold," was also destined to fail, as the Judge himself tripped up on the threshold of insobriety. Jim was eager to record its progress, remarking:

This organization is flourishing finely. It held a regular meeting last night, at which all the members were present except the President, for whom the Sergeant-at-arms was directed to inquire. After a long search, the delinquent officer was found asleep in Anderson's barn, and the whole Club went to take a look at him. "Fainted," says one, who had faith in the President's moral courage. "Came in here to have a quiet nap—was up all last night at work, you know," remarked a sympathizing member. By this time Fred Anderson, seeing the squad of reformers, and fearing that the hungry millionaires were making a raid on his beef, elbowed his way in until he stood astride the prostrate body of the leading reformer. "Dead?" he inquired, with a horrified look at the prone form of his friend. Then, falling upon his knees for closer scrutiny of the face by the dim light of a candle, he exclaimed, with considerable vehemence: "Dead be d——d! He's drunker'n a salivated horse-thief, and his breath smells like a puppy's nest." Then they all took a smell, and the conclusion was that their respected President was too drunk for anything. Mournfully they filed out of the barn to their clubroom, where they went into secret session, the proceedings of which we shall endeavor to obtain.

After such hamstrung attempts at reform, Townsend stepped forth with a sure cure of his own, stating: "A friend asks us if an old toper can be weaned from his bibulous practices. We say yes. The habit of drinking can be cured by giving the drinkers all the liquor they want to drink all the time. We know of two in our experience who were cured in three weeks. One jumped out of a four-story window and ran a curbstone into his head. The other didn't get up one morning and has now a curbstone growing over his head." This suggestion completely scattered the reformers, and Jim was forced to turn elsewhere for material to grace the pages of the *Index*.

As the snow deepened, however, times grew duller and duller and items scarcer, causing Jim to lament, "If any body thinks it's an easy job to hunt up local items in this howling wilderness let him try it on." But at last the arrival of Washington's Birthday offered a lively though brief reprieve.

The anniversary of Washington's birthday was royally celebrated in this canyon. Patriotism cropped out exuberantly, and manifested itself so heartily that the full-blooded American bubbled over with national pride and looked on with a watery eye—frequently so watery that he couldn't see the road. The celebration was inaugurated early in the day by a go-as-you-please procession from one saloon to another, the man who had the most money acting as Grand Marshal. By dark the crowd were ready to celebrate the birthday of anybody who would put up for the whisky. Though knives and pistols were plentifully displayed, very few deaths occurred, and those only when a gun went off accidentally while the celebrants were running each other around stoves and such obstructions as a man could dodge behind. Taken as a whole the day was one which should be forgotten as soon as possible.

The dullness was quick to return, however, and Jim was soon writing items out of such exciting stuff as a stalled bull team.

To be grand marshal of a bull-procession a man must have grace, patience, muscle, and a deep insight into bovine proclivities. Joe Curtis seems to possess all these qualifications. The other day, in a blinding snowstorm, his team was stalled on

Chicago Avenue, having an immense log in tow. Lookers-on went to his assistance, and each proceeded to pull out a big club. The grand marshal distributed his aids along the line of beef, and then waited for a lull in the storm, in order that the team might get the full sense of his exhortations which were to follow. A moment later the riot began: "Haw, Brigham!" "Gee, Star!" "Git, you — —!" And the marshal and his aids swore, and yelled, and jumped stiff-legged in a frenzy of anxiety to get that log to the mill; but not a thing moved—not even an ox stirred. The cattle quietly chewed their cuds and awaited the next shower of blows and curses. The drivers then held a consultation, after which each one seized a bull by the tail and stood waiting for the signal, like gunners holding lock-strings of a battery. When the word was given they set to twisting those tails, much as a Chinaman wrings out a wet blanket, and this concerted attack in the rear was more than the animals could stand. They lit out with a jerk which pulled the sled from under the log, which was left lying in the road, and is there still.

Or when nothing else was handy he had to make big doings of the untimely death of Wilcox's pig.

Wilcox took a notion the other day to start a hog-ranch. The speculation was suggested to him on observing a fine chance to steal a pig. He purloined the porker and packed it home. Next day piggy got sick. It had a bellyache and the blues, and the tip of its kinky little tail was cold as ice, and it no longer cheerfully grunted in response to kindly scratchings. There were heaps of trouble in that household then. Wilcox is not much of a doctor, though closely related to one, but he realized that something must be done. He said to himself: "I don't know much about anything 'cept fits—used to have 'em myself once, and I recollect what the folks did for me. Now, if I can give him something to set him into fits, and then doctor him for the blind staggers, I think I can save him." So he pounded up a lot of glass and bluestone and tamped it into the pig with an umbrella handle, and then stood aside to wait for the fits to come. Pretty soon the animal began to look blue around the gills; then it spewed up bluestone and broken glass, and flopped over and died, while Wilcox looked on and disconsolately murmured: "If he'd had only just one fit I'd a-cured him." A friend irritated him somewhat by remarking that it was a queer way to cure pork.

In February of 1881, Dan Jones closed down for good his weekly *Bentonian,* and that same month Bill Barnes suspended the Mammoth City *Herald.* They each crated up what few assets they had in their printing plants and struck out for Bodie to work for wages—though each intended to start a paper of his own again somewhere, as soon as fortune would permit. By mid-March Ed Everett had also had enough of publishing at Lundy and sold out to Townsend for credit—the only currency in circulation that winter. Jim's faith too in everything but equality was nearly worn through as he wrote, "Whoopee! hurrah for us wealthy people! We own a pig, wooly office dog, three chickens, a gourd of fat, and are milking a borrowed cow. We begin to feel like oppressing the poor, as other possessors of great wealth do, but our conscience restrains us."

Now, running the paper alone, Jim had little time even for inventing the news, and straight humdrum items started to fill up the local page. The only vent for his talents was through such occasional short quips as: "The biggest boom at the present is the one on Jack Hall's boat."

8

Round Men and Square Holes

SPRING'S RETURN made Townsend anxious also to get back into something more fruitful than the publishing business. During the winter he had joined wits with Col. Kikendale and assayer Wilcox to promote a mine, the Top Sawyer, which they had located on the eastern side of Lake Canyon. It was an ideal scheme and typical of the region; the Colonel was to try to sell the mine to any and every well-heeled stranger who came through the doors of the Snowflake Saloon, on the estimate of over $1500 a ton by Lundy's prominent assayer, W. A. Wilcox. The exuberant recommendations of Lundy's editor, J. W. E. Townsend, in the columns of the *Homer Mining Index* were to hail it as the "richest rock ever seen in camp." But whether the confederates ever unloaded this bonanza on an unwary capitalist is somehow lost to the records. Another venture, the Constellation Tunnel Company—the Sutro tunnel of the Homer District—was backed by the impressive association of Sheehy, Meacham, Brown, Townsend, Hallahan and Hallahan, but it never got beyond the stage of "preliminary work begun." Finally Jim fell back on his arrastra, which, with the aid of Ed Everett, he ran through most of the summer and early fall.

For some months, Townsend had been looking for someone to unload the *Index* on, and at last, about the end of July, he convinced John I. Ginn, the mining editor of the Bodie *Free Press* and an old acquaintance from Virginia City, to try his luck in Lundy. Ginn, two years Jim's senior, had come west from Georgia before the Civil War and had spent most of the intervening years on various Virginia City papers, including the *Old Piute, Trespass, Constitution*, and *Safeguard*. He had also occasionally wandered afield to work as local editor on such papers as the Treasure City *White Pine News*, the Winnemucca *Silver State* and the Oakland *Tribune*. In the fall of 1879 he came to Bodie to edit the Bodie *Standard*, and, when it failed the following summer, he became the mining editor of the *Free Press*. Ginn bought the *Index* on the first of August, and with the aid of Ferd Frost, a Bodie printer, he quickly turned the paper into a first-class mining journal, bulging with lengthy mining reviews every week.

Ginn also fancied himself an author and rehashed for the readers of the *Index* what he must have considered his finest literary piece, the tale of Tommy Mulligan's "Woild Noight on Treasure Hill," written a dozen years earlier for the *White Pine News*. Early the following year he outclassed even this masterpiece in a 7,000-word description of a barrage of avalanches, which burst down upon Lundy on what he might well have called a "Woild Woild Noight in Lundy Canyon." In restraint, however, he dubbed it simply "A Phenomenal Storm," from which we quote brief highlights as an instructive contrast to Townsend's methods.

At 4:30 P.M. on the 15th an avalanche of snow dropped from a cliff near the top of Mount Scowden, about 2,500 feet above Mill Creek and the southern portion of the town, struck upon a bench 800 feet below, bounded into the air and sailed 1,500 feet through space, settling down upon and crushing several dwellings and other houses that up to that time had been considered in the safest situation in the Canyon. A large number of men, armed with shovels, went to the rescue and soon succeeded in exhuming the people buried.

An hour afterward another avalanche came crashing down the high cliff on the north side of the canyon and immediately overlooking the most populous portion of the town. This came with a crash of trees, a grinding of rocks and a terrible rush of air before it, until it struck upon the projecting rock bench back of and above the May Lundy Hotel, when it burst into spray, filling the air with fine snow rushing with such velocity that it was driven into solid boards. . . .

Andy Nelson was sleeping in the toll house at the mouth of Lake Canyon when the procession of avalanches moved. A huge snow slide, starting from the top of Mount Gilcrest, rushed across the canyon, struck Mount Scowden, turned down Lake Canyon creek and ran to within 200 feet of Mill Creek—a total distance of one mile and a half. In its course it swept away a strong log stable at the toll house, a bale of hay, some barley, and an old gray horse that had been employed on the capstans drawing up the machinery for the Great Sierra tunnel at Tioga. Next morning Nelson went out to feed his horse, but could find neither horse nor feed. Procuring a long pole he commenced prospecting, and kept it up until a relief party going up Lake Canyon Creek, late in the afternoon, heard the old horse breathing under the snow. Digging in, they found him, in an upright position, like a soldier, with the feed by his side and two heavy logs of the stable resting across his nose. He was uninjured, barring a crick in his neck which keeps his head turned toward one shoulder—just fitting him for circular work, such as is required in turning a capstan.

At about the same hour as the other avalanches occurred, a thunder-bolt of snow struck the Trumble House, near the foot of the May Lundy tramway, in Lake Canyon, carrying away the building and scattering the wreck for a distance of 200 feet across the canyon. There were sleeping in the house at the

time Robert J. Trumble, Alex. McKeon, D. B. Grant, Henry
Schumaker, Christian Hablitzel and Steve Trumble. The first
four named were either killed outright or were subsequently
asphyxiated under the snow. Steve Trumble got out barefooted
and with nothing but his underclothing on, and through the
deep snow and bitter cold storm attempted to make Pat Regan's
cabin, some 300 feet distant. After wallowing in the snow for a
while, sometimes sinking over his head, and finding that his
feet were freezing, he procured two of the blankets in which he
had been sleeping, and by spreading first one and then the
other on the snow in front and crawling on his hands and knees,
he was finally enabled to approach near enough to the cabin to
alarm Regan's dog. Regan took him in, rubbed his feet with
snow until he brought the frost to the surface, and then visited
the scene of the disaster with a lantern. Nothing could be seen
save the great ridge of compact snow and here and there a fragment of building, and nothing could be heard save the thun-
ders of the storm.

IN LESS trying times Townsend dropped by and treated Ginn's
readers to more humorous pieces, such as his rendering of "Burkham's Circus."

On Thursday morning Fred. Anderson attempted to drive six
fat and frisky young beef cattle up to Tioga to slaughter for
the Great Sierra Mining Company. On reaching the tamarack
thicket near Lake Oneida, in upper Lake Canyon, the cattle
became unmanageable and scattered in the brush and rocks.
S. B. Burkham was in the vicinity at the time on horse-
back and volunteered his services to assist in getting the cattle
around the lake. A wild-eyed young heifer of the band was par-
ticularly fractious, and Burkham went for her with the remark,
"She's my meat"—but she wasn't and on the contrary she twice
came within a foot or two of reversing Burkham's order of exer-
cises. She took up a position on an elevated plateau and as
Burkham left his horse to "surround" her on foot, bystanders
observed that the shy young thing wrought an extra curl in her

switch and took a sly glance at him. As he approached her she suddenly arched her back like a courting cat, and went for him. The cloud of dust, rocks and flying tamarack tops shut out the conclusion of the scene, but after a while Burkham came cautiously creeping through the brush from the opposite direction, just as though he had been clear round the track and was lingering along for the heifer to come up and give him a brush on the home stretch. He mounted his trusty steed and hunted her up. She would not attack the horse but again took the brow of a steep little rise, where the horse could not follow. Burkham again dismounted and again approached her on foot. She stood just above a large log, and Burkham took the precaution as he approached to keep the log between them—but the heifer didn't; for suddenly Burkham heard something drop on his side of the log—and it was the heifer. A new idea seemed to have flashed across Burkham's mind, just at that moment, to the effect that he hadn't lost any heifer so he turned and started down the hill but suddenly found another log across his path. Over this he went, but in crossing it his head got ahead of his heels and he piled up in a heap below—just as the mad heifer cleared the log, Burkham and all, and went tearing through the brush like a cyclone in search of him. Of course she didn't find him and when she reached the meadow below she stopped and stared in a dazed sort of way at the lofty rock cliff to the east, as if in doubt whether she had not made a fool of herself by twice chasing a shadow. She looked up at her horns. There was no gore nor visible fragment of Burkham there. Then she dropped her tail, gently let out the kinks, and with a subdued air quietly walked back to the herd. It was now too late to reach Tioga before dark, even if the cattle would go without further trouble, and as by that time the wind was blowing a gale, Fred. Anderson turned about and drove the cattle back to his corral below town—Burkham waiting up the canyon till the grade was clear.

With such occasional help from Townsend, the *Index* remained a lively and readable paper for the few years that Ginn remained its editor and publisher. Townsend in the meantime had been taking his cut from the arrastras and amusing himself in local theatricals, Fourth of July orations, lectures and any other occasion he could find to speak. On one occasion, however, Ed Cleveland, editor of the Bodie *Free Press*, reported in his telegraphic items:

"Jim Townsend, the poet of Mill Creek, has not spoken a word for sixty minutes, on a wager of keeping silent for twenty-four consecutive hours. His pulse is regular and there is every indication of his ultimate recovery. All Mill Creek witnessed the phenomenon." But one hour appears to have been Jim's limit for he found that no amount of money was worth being deprived of hearing his own voice.

Cleveland in his mid-twenties took evident delight in pulling "Old Jim's" leg. He achieved his greatest triumph that October when he ran an item, "No Place For A Cat."

Jim Townsend of Lundy has been making some experiments with an ordinary domestic cat. It has been repeatedly stated that a cat could not live at an altitude of 13,000 feet above the sea. Mr. Townsend has demonstrated the fact that such is a fact. On Monday last he and another gentleman made the ascent of Castle Peak which is a little over 13,000 feet high. They took with them a cat—Thomas—that was a year old and had lived at an altitude of 6,000 feet with no symptoms of disease. Mr. Townsend had the cat in a box and as they went up he took observations and noted very carefully every movement of the feline. When the summit was reached they pitched their tent; this was about 2 o'clock in the afternoon. The cat partook of some food and after playing for an hour or so fell asleep and did not wake up until near midnight. When it did recover consciousness, it set up a howling and appeared much distressed. Townsend pitied it and endeavored to make it feel at home; but no use. It kept up its constant moaning and displayed symptoms of having fits. When morning came the cat was offered food, but it refused to eat, and acted even more strange than during the night. Townsend says it would open its mouth as if gasping for breath; would jump about, then go to sleep and wake up with a start. All this while close watch was kept and every movement noted. At 3 o'clock in the afternoon the cat died of exhaustion.

The story hit its mark and Townsend swore that as soon as the snow drove him down to the "White settlements" he was going to Bodie to "get after the Gothic nose of Cleveland." But when they did meet again Cleveland doubtless treated to a round and all was forgiven.

BY LATE summer Dan Jones was done with working for wages again and loaded up his make-shift printing plant to found a newspaper at Hawthorne, Nevada, the newly established terminus of the Carson and Colorado Railroad—some thirty miles northeast of Bodie. There on September 1, 1881, he launched the weekly *Oasis*. As the title indicates, Dan had, as usual, unbridled his optimism for the future of the town, because the howling sand and sagebrush waste that was Hawthorne could in no way remotely resemble an oasis.

A townsite had been sketched out on the sand in April, and after five months little more than a dozen clapboard shanties marked its progress. Yet Jones was a dauntless booster, and with the second number of the *Oasis* he single-handedly led a campaign to draw the Esmeralda county seat away from its spacious brick quarters in Aurora to a dusty canvas tent at Hawthorne. Despite the absurdity of the suggestion the Aurora *Esmeralda Herald* bristled, and a lively county seat war raged on paper for a full month.

But all too soon what little money Jones had brought with him ran out, and with its sixth number on October 6 he suspended the *Oasis*, lamenting:

This is a world of sadness. It becomes the sad duty of the undersigned to announce that with this issue his connection with the *Oasis*, either as editor or manager, ceases. What may be the disposition of the paper hereafter will be the subject of a future announcement. The enterprise started as an experiment, and the experiment so far as this affiant is concerned, is a failure. It may be possible to publish a newspaper on one square meal a week; but to undertake to do so on one square a month, and hash only once in thirty-one days for the long months is a little more than human nature can stand. It might be done in Missouri but it will prove a dead failure in Nevada. Hawthorne has a future before it, and we look for the building up of an inland town here of considerable importance. But printers, as a rule, are not wealthy enough to run newspapers for glory. If the *Oasis* should not be continued by other parties, and is really dead, it cannot be said that its life, though brief, was jolly. To those friends who have endeavored to aid the enterprise by patronage and encouragement we return our sincere thanks. Liberty and Nevada. Ta ta.

—Orlando E. Jones.

Yet brief as the venture was, Dan's efforts had not gone unsung, for even the Virginia City *Territorial Enterprise* regretted its passing:

It is not a little strange that half the time, and more than half the time, round men are attracted to and try to fit themselves into square holes. This thought is brought up by the recent experience of our old friend Dan (Orlando) Jones in his newspaper venture at Hawthorne. Dan produced a spicy little paper (the *Oasis*) which everyone wished to see live and flourish, but it died. Dan was a round man with everyone, but he got into a square hole. This is not the first nor the second time this has happened. Dan has started half a dozen papers. He has made them all bright; has made them all such papers as newspaper men in general desired to see live, but Dan has always, round as he is, got into a square hole. We earnestly hope that when he turns loose again it may be in a place that will fit him on all sides.

Once again Dan packed up his paraphernalia and returned to Bodie, where Bill Barnes had been making plans to resurrect the ghost of his former Mammoth City *Herald* under the name of the Bodie *Evening Herald*. Barnes had moved his press over from Mammoth in June, but it still had several attachment suits hanging on it from his creditors. After a number of financial false starts, Barnes at last announced that the money was forthcoming and he would commence the *Evening Herald* for certain on December 19. But the 19th came and passed and soon even December had passed and no *Herald* enlivened Bodie's evening hours.

But Dan Jones had already succeeded in locating another square hole, having also taken a fancy to try to start a paper in Bodie. On January 2, 1882, he shook out his new sheet, the weekly *Opinion*. The *Opinion* was to be the Democratic organ for all of Mono County, and Ed Cleveland of the thoroughly Republican *Daily Free Press*, feeling no threat to his own interests, paid the diminutive paper good notice, complimenting Jones as a "graceful writer" and predicting that the "Weekly *Opinion* will soon be very popular." Popular it certainly was, but successful it was not—and for survival it needed to be both. It folded after the third or fourth issue, just as Barnes once again took off for San Francisco to get the money to start his paper.

When Barnes returned the following week without the cash, he was even more dejected than before, and, finding his wife taking care of L. E. Tubbs, a sick friend, in a locked hotel room, he pulled a British bull-dog pistol and let fire. Tubbs was winged in the leg and hit once in the chest, or rather in his watch. He recovered within a few days and Barnes was jailed for a month until the case was dropped. The following month, after Barnes had failed in a final effort to raise the money to redeem his printing plant, Justice Thomas Newman took over the material—though Barnes refused to recognize the transaction.

Judge Newman was not interested in having the press lie idle, and about the first of May, leased it to John Curry and Dan Jones. Curry, one of the founders of the *Homer Mining Index*, had been slinging type for the *Esmeralda Herald* and was eager to have a paper of his own again. Jones was also eager to resume publishing, but he felt some guilt about using Barnes's material. Curry had no qualms, however, so they adopted the firm name of John J. Curry & Co., hoping that Barnes might not learn of Dan's connection with the paper. On May 8, 1882, they launched a new daily, the Bodie *Evening Miner*, not mentioning that Jones was both co-lessee and editor. But it was already too late, for John Ginn had heralded the paper two days earlier in the *Homer Mining Index*—giving much attention to its editor, Dan Jones, whom he recommended as "a forcible and facile writer, possessing a versatility of wit rarely equaled, and will make the columns of the *Miner* chatoyant as precious opals set in jet." In praise or not, the secret was out, and as Dan had expected Barnes was outraged.

The *Miner* was "as independent as a hog on ice, but with strong Democratic leanings." Being a daily it could compete with the *Free Press*, which it also equaled in size. In recognition of this, Cleveland extended no welcome to the *Miner* as he had to the *Opinion*, but instead ominously warned that there was no room in Bodie for two dailies. After four years of journalistic squabbling between the two papers, the *Free Press* prediction was to be fulfilled, but it was Dan's *Miner* that won out, for Dan had at last found a round hole.

When he was sober, Bill Barnes simply refused to speak to Jones or even recognize the existence of the *Miner* office, but after making the rounds of Bodie's saloons he felt loaded for action. Finally, on the first of August, he got to thinking how nearly nine years ago to the day he had first hauled that press across the desert to Columbus, Nevada, to start the *Borax Miner*, and how fond he had become of it in the intervening years. He decided once and for all that he had to act—and he struck out down the street for the *Miner* office. But what followed is best described by the *Free Press* reporter.

Tuesday afternoon W. W. Barnes made a raid on the *Evening Miner* office with disastrous results, both to the standing type in that office and to his own head. Mr. Barnes was once the owner of the type, press, etc., which is employed in printing that paper, and he claims to be the owner of it still. . . . He is especially emphatic upon this point when under the influence of liquor, as was his condition Tuesday, when he entered the *Miner* office. He walked up to the frame where the genial Dan Jones was at the time "setting out of his head" some specially fine items, and in a careless way tipped over a whole galley of type. Upon request to leave the sacred precincts of the sanctum, he complied, but on the way out he seized the fourth page form and hauled it off the imposing stone, and had the first page nearly off before he could be restrained. Mr. Curry went off and had a warrant issued for Barnes' arrest, but while he was absent the irate ex-publisher returned. Justice Thomas Newman, who is now the owner of the material, was in the office on this occasion. He warned Barnes against doing further damage, who replied that this was his own office and he could do what he pleased with it. He (Newman) had stolen the office, but it belonged to himself (Barnes). He is charged with following up his remarks by striking Judge Newman, who, notwithstanding the disadvantage of a wooden leg, is mighty lively in a "scrap" fight. The Judge struck out with a short stick, and soon had his adversary a fit subject for the doctor, Barnes being considerably bruised about the head and bleeding profusely. He was subsequently arrested on a charge of malicious mischief, and will be brought before Justice Phlegar for trial.

Barnes was again released and remained in Bodie two more years attempting to regain his press by more legal means, before he finally left in disgust for Los Angeles.

9

The New Boss Liar
of the Universe

IN LATE November of 1881, just before the first heavy snows of the season choked off the high passes of the Sierra, Jim Townsend made a clean-up on the arrastra, settled his affairs at Lundy and headed west over the mountains to the old camps of Tuolumne, where he once mined. With his jaw moving "at a rate of forty miles an hour" he negotiated his line of bull into free whisky at the watering places of Tuolumne county, and as his jaw lost currency he drifted north along the Mother Lode in easy style through Calaveras, Amador, Eldorado and Placer counties. He was well remembered along this route; the Angels Camp *Mountain Echo* advised its readers simply: "That man from Mono has been sojourning among us for a few days. . . . He has the usual sixty years' experience of a forty-year-old man, and tells some remarkable stories of that famous country." Thus he continued throughout the winter.

When he reached Auburn in early spring, Townsend concluded to catch the train east, back over the Sierra to Washoe, rather than offer himself up to the lingering sentiments of his old acquaintances in Grass Valley a short distance to the north.

In the early 1880s Reno was the fastest growing town in Nevada, for in that decade its population tripled while every other major town in the state declined. The townsite had been laid out in the spring of 1868 with the completion of the Central Pacific Railroad across the Sierra. Its immediate growth came from the abandonment of nearby Washoe City, and its later development stemmed from its importance as the transshipping point to the Comstock. By 1882 its population of roughly fifteen hundred read two rival dailies, the *Nevada State Journal* and the *Evening Gazette*.

Shortly after Townsend arrived in Reno, he wandered into the *Gazette* office and there was offered the local columns of the paper by its publisher, Robert Fulton, who was already aware of Jim's facility for flushing news items where no sober man could find them. Jim quickly accepted and, fortified with a couple of shots of whisky, set about to cook up enough local items to fill out the *Gazette's* portion of three to four columns daily. The local citizenry, however, gave him neither aid nor comfort, and he howled:

A reporter is not ubiquitous, nor has he eyes all over him like a potatoe. He has a sort of negative right to ask folks if they "know anything going on," and when he gets a surly answer he jots it down in the blackbook of his memory against the illbred swine who snubs him, for he knows that a day of retribution will surely come, when he can pile coals of fire upon the heads of those who decline to give a civil answer to a gentlemanly question. It is singular that these same reticent hogs think more of a local item than any other men do. If one of them becomes the father of a scrawny baby with a mouth big enough to feed with a fire shovel, he wants the reporter to say it is a beautiful ten-pounder, with flowing hair and a full set of teeth.

But things were not nearly so bad as they first appeared, for Townsend soon discovered that Reno had one tremendous advantage over such places as Antioch and Lundy—one guaranteed news item every day in the arrival of the transcontinental trains. And what more could a local reporter desire when a whole trainload of assorted and insultable eastern freaks paraded through daily to be exhibited in the local columns of his paper. Jim did well by them, too, working hard to ferret out the peculiarities of each to feed the columns of the *Gazette*. As a result the paper enjoyed such xenophobic fare as the following items:

A Boston Female

A young lady of doubtful age, supposed to have hailed from Boston, and a passenger on the west-bound overland last night, jumped out of the sleeper and made a rush for the Depot Hotel dining room that would have made a Washoe Indian squaw blush with shame. She dropped into a chair and gobbled up a chunk of bread about the size of her foot and gulped it down at one swallow. She was one of the kind that would have made four bites of a strawberry if she had had one and knew that anyone was looking at her. After satisfying her ravenous appetite, she left the table, walked out on the platform and put on more aesthetic airs than a country stud-horse. It is quite interesting to watch the Bostonians when they arrive here. Some of them make for a saloon the first thing, while others gobble up more of Chamberlain's grub for 75 cents than six hardy wood-choppers would in two meals. They go for beans like Pat Kelly's ducks for corn.

You Can't Fool Them

Frequenters of the depot can tell a Bostonian by his actions. He appears to be upset all the time. He has paid his money to ride on the cars between two places, and he will never leave them for an instant unless they are at a standstill. He jumps off the train for a ten-cent lunch, but if there is any switching done, which is frequently necessary, he bounces aboard in tremulous haste, revolving in his mind how he shall most economically make reclamation upon the railroad company for the coffee he left in his cup. He wants all that he has paid for, and as much more as he can pack off or experience. The morning express at Reno is split in two and the "Carson Sleeper" taken out and side-tracked, during which operation the head of the train makes several movements up and down the track. The instant the locomotive commences to blow the condensed steam from its cylinders, preparatory to starting, the Bostonians jump aboard, and will get on to the engine if no car is attached, and ride up and down the track for half an hour, notwithstanding the fact that they are told there is plenty of time and that the conductor will give a distinct signal in time for all passengers to leisurely board the cars.

The Bold Ben Gets Sold

Ben Graves, the most oily of the oily fraternity of news agents, is generally sharp enough for the boys, but they manage to take him into camp once in a while. The other day the porter and one of the brakemen put up a little job that he fell into entirely. They took the glass out of an Arizona diamond pin, and threw it down by the stove, and when Ben came through the car were talking excitedly about one of the passengers in one of the sleepers who had just lost a diamond out of his ring. Ben joined in the search for it, and was allowed to find it. After the passengers got off the boys tried to buy it off him, and ran up the bids from fifteen to thirty-eight dollars. He refused to sell his treasure, but had it examined next day by Goeggel, the jeweler, who informed him that its commercial value was less than a short bit.

A Pugnacious Touress

A ponderously fleshy woman boarded the train between Reno and Winnemucca yesterday, and when Ben Sargent, the slim and angular conductor, went to collect fare, she wanted to palm off a lot of brass jewelry as collateral for her ride. Ben said that wouldn't pay the company, and declined to receive the plunder. At Lovelock's he tried to put her off, but she wouldn't be dumped into the Great American Desert without protest. The result was a most interesting scrimmage between a very slim conductor and a very fat train-jumper. She smashed a window and a glass door, and was apparently about to throw the car off the track, when a freight conductor came up to assist Ben in the dumping process. She didn't relish the interference, and asked the meddlesome marshal of a cattle-train "what he had to do with it." Then she caressed him in the pit of the stomach with a No. 9 kip, and he sauntered to his caboose and sung out "all aboard." Finally a brakeman came to Ben's assistance, and together they emptied her out of the car. When the trouble was over and everything quiet, she walked up to an innocent-looking bystander and benumbed him with a blow on the jaw. Then she began to wreck the station-house windows, and it was feared she would tear up the track. The agent telegraphed to Wadsworth to know what to do, and was told to "take a club and welt the stuffing out of her."

But on rare occasions a real celebrity would arrive, such as Eli Perkins [Melville D. Landon], the popular eastern humorist, braggadocio and protégé of Artemus Ward. When his train languished for an hour in Reno in May of 1882, all the Washoe reporters turned out to interview him. But the interview had scarcely started when Townsend, not to be outdone, began to drown him out with a deluge of his own. Robert Fulton wrote up the tourney the following day under the caption: "Eli Perkins, The Boss Liar of the Universe Cleaned Out by a 'Gazette' Reporter."

Eli Perkins, the humorist, passed through Reno last evening, en route to San Francisco. While the train was waiting here he was introduced to Jim Townsend. After the usual introductory salutation Jim declared himself as follows:

"I have often heard of you, Mr. Perkins, but hardly think I have met you before."

"I know you very well, Mr. Townsend, by reputation. I met an old gentleman in New York years ago, who, I remember, was called lying Jim Townsend. It seems to me you resemble him somewhat. Do you know him sir?" inquired the humorist.

"What sir?" replied Jim, who is as deaf as a post when he wants to be.

"Did you ever meet lying Jim Townsend?"

"Oh, yes, indeed I have known him for over 60 years. He was a rascally prevaricator. No relation of mine, however," was Jim's mild reply.

"You have been a resident of the coast for several years, have you not, Mr. Townsend?" inquired Eli.

"Yes. I came here in '45 the first time, in company with John C. Fremont, and was acting as his guide, when he repelled an attack by Mexicans near Monterey in March, '46, and I might add, Mr. Perkins, by way of parenthesis, that the world owes the discovery of California gold to James W. E. Townsend, and 'don't you forget it,' Mr. Marshall to the contrary not withstanding."

"Can you tell me —"

"Yes sir," said Townsend, interrupting. "I can tell you anything you want to know about the discovery of gold or the Mexican war. I was a Captain in that bloody conflict. Well, as I was about to remark, after getting Fremont and his party through, I returned East and shipped from Boston in the sailing vessel Venice, as first mate, landing on the golden shore for the second time in early '49, and made a half a million before the good old year slipped out of her Fall suit, took my dust, went to San Jose, and started the first printing press that ever turned a wheel on the coast, and it is going now. I took a liking to the business, and was at one time on the old Sacramento *Union*. I put in many a hard night's work on the dear old *Union*. Why, dammit, man, I've had 28 compositors howling for 'copy' at one time, and not a damned scribbler in the editorial room but me."

"Did you —"

"Yes, I should say so. I have started 23 papers on this coast and they are all alive yet. Why, man! I built the first quartz mill ever put up in Asia. I am the man who told Mark Twain the story of the jumping frog of Calaveras county. Why, dammit! I published it before Mark Twain was born. I —," but at this interesting period of Captain Jim's history, 'a dull heavy thud' was heard in the sleeper, and upon examination poor Perkins was found as stiff as a poker in the aisle of the car. A mutual friend pulled Townsend off and started with him up town. "Why," says Jim, "I raised Eli Perkins, and can tell him more about California than anybody. If I didn't forget to tell him about starting Claus Spreckles in the sugar business on the Sandwich Islands, I'm a liar."

SEVERAL months later Townsend had the opportunity to repeat this performance when the Marquis of Lorne, Governor General of the Dominion of Canada, and his wife, the princess Louise, daughter of Queen Victoria, were passing through Reno on their way to British Columbia. Jim lost no time telling the marquis "that he had sixteen arrastras running in Mill Creek Canyon; that Bodie had a population of 13,000 inhabitants and that he was the Lord Mayor of the place; . . . that he came around the horn in '48; that he was the first miner to find gold in Nevada County; that he was the mate of a merchant vessel when only fourteen years of age; that when it came to mining he did not take a back seat to any man; that he had forgotten more about mining than nine-tenths of all the superintendents in Nevada and California knew; that he was a good doctor and a first-class assayer; that he had the newspaper business by the heart; that he was about to write a book and that he was soon going East on a lecture tour." At this point the train moved on, and the marquis fell into the arms of Princess Louise. When he recovered, however, he telegraphed back to the leading photographer in Reno, asking that he send him a picture of Townsend, which he might "place among his collection of remarkable men."

Most of the time, however, Townsend had to write up the news rather than make it, and when the trains failed to bring him news he would take a sharp jab at the railroads themselves.

The eastern railroad companies do all in their power to make their employees happy and contented. An aromatic car-coupler has been invented. It consists chiefly of a rubber bag filled with cologne, and when the cars come together the bag is pressed, and fifty cents worth of delicious odor is thrown over the brakeman. This is done by the railroad companies to show their appreciation and gratitude to the brakeman, who frequently shows his devotion to his employer by throwing himself under a car wheel and being jammed to death like a Hindoo devotee of Juggernaut.

Townsend seldom gave the locals a rest from laughing at themselves. His researches into native infirmities turned up, among other things, a rare case of "sheep-jiggles," and this is followed by accounts of other curious Washoe customs:

A man at the Palace this morning attracted considerable attention by his strange and incomprehensible gestures. His jaw vibrated like a fiddle-string, and every now and then he dropped a small stone from one hand to the other. No one could imagine what was the matter with him until a well-known sheep-raiser entered and, in apparent surprise, accosted him: "Hello, Jake! When did you get here?" But there was no response. Then a light seemed to break in on the sheep man, and he exclaimed: "Good Lord! folks, this man's got the sheep-herder's jiggles. He went out here a week ago to count a band of sheep. There wasn't more than a thousand in the bunch, but he's been counting them ever since, till he's cross-eyed and dazed, and can see nothing but sheep. You know when we count 'em we let 'em jump through an opening just big enough for one at a time, and as they come we count till we get up to a hundred, and then drop a stone from one hand to the other and commence afresh. He's been doing this for a week, and can't see anything but sheep now from here to Wadsworth."

Townsend turned his attention also to the customs of both red men and white as a source of humor. His evenhanded racism never let either get a monopoly on dignity, or even much of a glimpse of it.

A Piute Giantess

A squaw can pack more than the average mule. What would rupture the kidneys of a Mill Creek jackass would just about ballast a Piute matron. This morning in the plaza a stout buck was loading up his squaw for a tramp. He piled a lot of blankets and baskets upon her back, and started her. On one side she towed a clumsy Newfoundland dog that wasn't broke to lead well, and it pulled back. On the other side she had a fat boy five or six years old. The dog wouldn't come along and the boy wouldn't go without it. The buck solved the problem at once by pitching the dog into one basket and the boy into another to balance things, and the caravan started, with the big buck in the rear, sweating under the weight of a linen duster, smoking a cigarette, and not a bit concerned whether his darling wife was staggering under half a ton or only three hundred pounds.

DANCING

Though dancing is a popular amusement the world over, there are comparatively few really graceful dancers. Many of the young men of Reno are good dancers, but some of them gyrate around a ball-room floor like a tumble-bug on a hot plate. Some men are pitiful sights when they get up to dance. Awkwardness is no name for their clumsy movements. The timid dancer first looks scared and then gets red-faced and reckless and fans the floor with his feet as if he had secreted something in a knot hole and were covering it with surrounding dirt. Sometimes he is about four bars ahead of the music, and then as far behind. He spasmodically clutches his partner, who feels as if she were jammed between two freight cars. He holds his breath till he bursts off his collar button and then blows off steam with a prolonged grunt. When the dance is over he stands paralyzed and dizzy for a moment, while the room seems to revolve like a turn-table. When he reaches a seat he flops down like a gob of mud and turns to swabbing the back of his neck with a handkerchief or fumbling with the button of his vest, which perhaps has become so displaced by his violent exertions as to expose a white gash of shirt across his abdomen.

Occasionally the local "news" might be so meagre that Jim used it only to introduce yarns from his own sizable store. The following bit of unnatural Natural History rises almost to poignancy.

SCARED TO DEATH

The locomotive about here that has a shriek like a Bodie keno dealer is a holy terror to horses. But one animal in particular it seems to fascinate. Every time this horse gets loose he quietly goes to a spot at a safe distance from the noisy monster, and patiently waits for it to come along, as it does every day about noon. He can tell it from all the other engines, and when it gives out one of its blood-curdling yells, the poor animal breaks out into a cold sweat and shivers like a dog adrift on an iceberg. If he does not get his regular dose of scare every day he is like an old opium-smoker without his pipe. He becomes contrary and balky and won't pull a pound until his owner drives him along Third street to hear the wild engine yell. This is a queer freak, certainly. But cats and dogs are frequently fascinated by things that frighten them, and a monkey will always fool around where he is likely to get scared. In the early days, a Tuolumne miner had a pet monkey. In the house was a box containing a toy jumping-jack. When the catch of the cover was loosed a hideous figure would spring up a foot or more. The monkey one day got to fumbling about the box, when up jumped the jack and down went Mr. Monkey in a cataleptic fit. There was sorrow and grief in that humble house until Jocko revived. It took hours of treatment with poultices and peppermint injections, and there was a very sick monkey for some days. As soon as he got well enough to crawl he climbed to a high shelf and went to fumbling again with that box, mournfully chattering and wheezing as he felt around for the catch. His inquisitiveness resulted in another fit. A few weeks afterward he became too weak to stand the shock, and died immediately after taking his favorite stimulant, having literally scared himself to death.

Reno life provoked Townsend on occasion to expose more fully his serious side, and change his tone from light mockery to sour irony on those who would profit from the great democracy of death.

"Undertaking" is a disagreeable business, but there are lots of money in it. A solid rosewood coffin built of redwood at a cost of a few dollars is disposed of to an afflicted family for a sum so large as to absorb the entire property of a deceased person and leave nothing for his heirs. For that reason the enterprising undertaker is on the lookout for business. He attends church, and keenly surveys the faces of the congregation with a critical eye. When prayer is requested by solicitous friends of a sick person for restoration to health, the undertaker "coppers" the invocation, and slipping away nimbly, deftly tucks his business card under the door of the invalid. He is jolly when pneumonia gallops through a community, and howls with delight over a wholesale railroad accident. He can diagnosis a case of physical degeneracy of any kind with unerring certainty at a distance of fifty feet. He will look at a man in the incipient stages of consumption and appoint his funeral to the day and hour, and the corpse is generally ready. He knows the dimensions of every man in the community, and the coffins he furnishes are always guaranteed to fit, so that the defunct customer can rest without danger of contracting chafes and bunions. But the far-seeking undertaker sometimes gets fooled, like ordinary people. For instance: When it was reported on the Comstock that a number of men were imprisoned in a drift in the Alta mine, and were dead to a certainty, a Virginia [City] undertaker telegraphed to San Francisco for six coffins, to be sent up by express in hot haste. The caskets arrived in Reno this morning and were immediately shipped to Virginia. When the undertaker heard that the men in the drift were not dead, he was doubtless stirred with tumultuous reflections over the reckless expense he had incurred in anticipation of a harvest of fat fees which he will not get.

TOWNSEND had scarcely settled down in Reno when he got the urge to ramble again. And early in July he took a couple of months' leave from his *Gazette* post and caught the stage south to Bodie. He told everyone he had to go back to set his arrastras grinding again on the rich ore from his mines. John Ginn, who looked in vain for both, dismissed them as "airy fabrics of his nimble and versatile fancy." Jim was appropriately outraged and announced that he would come gunning for Ginn, whereupon

John Dormer of the Candelaria *True Fissure* fearfully predicted that when Jim "reaches the dangerous canyon of the snowbound Mill Creek there will be a land slide, the component parts of which will be principally antimony, old iron, editor, racks and cases, and such other debris as may be found in any well regulated printing office."

But Ginn sagely averted the calamity by taking an immediate and extended excursion into the remote fastness of the High Sierra to make his first "annual" report on mining activity there. Ferd Frost, his compositor, was left behind to explain: "Hearing that James Wimbledon Ebenezer Townsend, Esq., the 'original Jacob' who won imperishable fame as Superintendent of King Solomon's mines in the Ormus and Ind, the trusted navigating officer of Columbus' flotilla, the pioneer petrologist of Jackass Hill, and the Eli Perkins of Pacific coast journalism, had arrived in Bodie and was expected in Lundy this week, the editor of the INDEX 'lit out' before daylight last Tuesday morning for the high Sierra, expecting to touch the telegraph line at Yosemite on Friday for information relative to the demolition of the INDEX office because the typos would insist upon having it that 'Jim's arrastras are the airy fabrics of his nimble and versatile fancy.'"

10

Fourteen Cats
in Fifteen Minutes

JIM TOWNSEND swung off the stage at Bodie with a new companion, a mutt named Jackson, that he had adopted as his mascot in Reno. Jackson was an immediate hit, and Jim touted him as the greatest thing that God ever put on four legs and a sure death to cats. But Ed Cleveland and the *Free Press* typos chose to withhold their praise till Jackson could be put to a test, something they immediately set out to do. As Cleveland recounted a few days later,

When he came over from Reno, Jim Townsend brought with him a dog. This animal, who sails under the weight of the name "Jackson," is a sort of an overgrown, black-and-tan with a bulldog head and an overshot under jaw. The waste basket of the FREE PRESS office is Jack's bunk house, and he eats every time the bell rings for the compositors. On the sunset side of Mono street dwells a female cat, and her family of three kittens. This motherly feline has for two years vexed with mirth the drowsy ear of Bodie night on the fence around the backyard of the Occidental and done a bareback ride through Broken-barrel avenue on every cur who has had the temerity to venture into this vicinity. Her caudal adornment is somewhat disfigured, it having been struck by a bullet from the self-cocker of a Mono House lodger, who fired onto the stage during the performance of a free concert on the roof of a cabin fronting on Main street.

Friday afternoon Jim was relating to the prints the amount of cat execution contained in Jack's overshot jaw.

"Why he killed 14 cats in 15 minutes the day after he had his leg broke in a scrap fight with the slaughter-house bull-dog," Jim told the boys in a confident tone and in his characteristically truthful manner.

"A wild cat stands no show with him, and he shakes a porcupine over the ropes in exactly two minutes and a half, railroad time."

Jim gave out several other pointers on his dark complexioned canine and then went down town to "set his watch." During the absence of the Renoite the aforementioned cat was brought over on a visit by a friend of Mr. Townsend's and when he returned five minutes later with Jack at his heels the latter descried the combative feline and began to show signs of uneasiness. Jim also saw the cat, and telling the crowd to stand back and give the Washoe county dog plenty of room, gave Jack the "office" to begin.

Jackson drew a bead through the sights on the end of his nose at the bob-tailed target and made a spring. The cat rose like an inflated balloon and, when the dog landed where she had stood, came down on his back. For a minute the air was full of yells and fur of Jim Townsend's dog, and while Jim was demanding in loud tones for him to "come off" and "quit it," Jack was vainly endeavoring to get a foothold on the floor or effect an exit through the side of the house and finally managed to reach the door and pass out and strike off down the street. The victorious cat shook Jack at the corner and trotted back to her roost, none the worse apparently for the fun she had. Jim found Jack under a sidewalk on Main Street and brought him back for repairs. Jim still swears that "that was the first cat Jackson ever tackled that he didn't wipe out in less than a minute."

THIS debacle elicited such choice comment from his friends that Jim is said to have packed up Jackson and departed on the first stage for Lundy. There presumably he searched patiently for John Ginn and his arrastras for about two weeks before he dared show his face in Bodie again. But no sooner had they returned than poor hapless Jackson heaped more odium upon the good name of his master and champion. Ed Cleveland eagerly publicized his misadventures, writing,

Sunday afternoon one of the boys took Jackson for a walk in the vicinity of the slaughter house. About the first break the dog made after arriving at this well known out-of-town resort was to roll himself well in the carcass of a decaying cow, and about the next was for home, followed by divers boulders and the select Chinook of his late friend.

Shortly after Mr. Townsend's champion light-weight Washoe county side-hold scrap fighter took the back track for his lodging and eating apartments in the *Free Press* building, the attention of families living along Union street was called to a large-size black-and-tan dog going down that thoroughfare. The aroma which trailed along behind him floated out upon the breezy atmosphere, and sailed in through open windows and doors, crowding all the fresh air apparently out of the neighborhood.

Passing through Union to Main street, Jackson's appearance created a profound sensation on that county road, and it was not more than a minute before he made a casino sweep of every man on the four sidewalks. He did not stop to press the business, but kept up his stunning gait, until the friendly shelter of the compositors' frame in the *Free Press* office had covered his retreat. His presence in the composing room was not known when he first entered, and it was not until his perfume began to thaw and penetrate all corners of the house, that suspicions arose in the minds of all present that a very strong practical joke was being perpetrated on them and they proceeded to investigate the matter on the outside, where a little fresh air yet remained. They soon convinced themselves that the whilom

Reno cat-exterminator was the foundation of the cause, and immediately scattered the nuisance once more in the direction of Main street.

Jim Townsend was standing on the principal promenade about this time talking to an old lady acquaintance, and, as is his wont, was telling the many virtues of his canine wonder and wishing him in sight, so that she might see the darling. He had just finished telling how in Reno Jackson used to keep three fights running all the time, and, as a specimen of his endurance, how he once ran a greyhound to death to get a bone the latter possessed, when he saw the object of his conversation in the vicinity of the Mono House.

Assuming the pose of an old settler pointing out the graveyard to a tenderfoot, Jim buried one hand to the hilt in his rear left pants pocket and extended the other five full toward Jackson with the remark "Ah, I see my little boy now. He sees me too and here he comes." So Jackson did come but before he got within shotgun range the lady was going in the direction of Van Voorhies' drug store, and Jim had one hand on his nose and was motioning with the other for his little boy to go to the devil, or some other secluded rendezvous. Jackson became morose under so much harsh treatment and crawled into the town sewer on Main street, from which place, and for two dollars, a Piute removed him to the Standard pond and gave him a renovation. Mr. Townsend spent Monday with a long gun in search of the man who gave Jackson his coat of smell.

JIM LEFT by stage for Aurora a few days later without his canine companion. But Jim's old Bodie comrades came to Jackson's rescue and immediately took up a collection to put him on the next stage out. One could not flee a more humane society.

It was late August, and after a few days in Aurora and Candelaria, Jim and Jackson returned to Reno. There Townsend resumed intermittent work on the *Gazette*, dealing out such wisdom as "Never lay down a hand when you have money to back up a bluff." In his extensive spare time he delivered a lecture, entitled "God Knows," wrote a little hymn for camp meetings, called "Squeeze Me a Little Tighter," and began work on a new story, "Ten Nights in Jerusalem," which he proposed to illustrate with more than a hundred patent medicine cuts. Thus he rounded out his literary endeavors for the season.

For the next two years Jim wintered in Washoe and summered in the Sierra, and in brief fits, as in the fall of 1882, he gave John Ginn a hand on the *Index*, adding a new chapter to his earlier tales of judicial proceedings with "An Accommodating Court."

A case of misdemeanor has been before Judge C. C. McLean for several days and has attracted a great deal of attention. Three or four venires have been issued and the whole township ransacked for jurymen. Justice McLean is a very patient and accommodating court. On Wednesday morning court convened at the usual hour, when it was ascertained that one of the subpoenaed was absent. An officer was dispatched for the delinquent, and soon afterward made return that the embryo juror was at breakfast and desired a recess of Court till he got through with his morning meal. Court took a recess—whereupon another juryman slipped away to get his noon breakfast, and the Court took a second recess to await his return. Finally the panel was exhausted without obtaining a full jury, and a new venire was issued. Late in the afternoon the officer served the paper on four men who were deeply absorbed in a game of 7-up for $1 a corner. The game had just begun—and it was continued without intermission for 38 hours. Soon after ten o'clock next forenoon an officer was dispatched after the four delinquents and he found them still absorbed in the game. They asked the officer to explain the situation to the Court and on their behalf request an adjournment until next day. Court adjourned and yesterday the 7-uppers responded to the roll-call and the case went on as though nothing had happened.

But by far his tallest tale of that season was the strange case of Ah Wee and "His Third Death."

Last week Jim Toy, the Celestial restaurateur of Lundy, received intelligence that his countryman and friend, Ah Wee, the pioneer laundryman of Bennettville, was sick unto death.

Jim hastened to the bedside of his dying friend, reaching his destination but a few minutes before Ah Wee expired. After the body became cold and rigid Jim went up to the boarding house for his supper, after which several parties accompanied him back to the laundryman's shanty—and it was well they did, for Ah Wee was up and walking about, and it required the united strength of the whole party to get him back to bed and to hold him there. Jim remained at his bedside administering such remedies as he thought the case required (Jim is a physician) but all to no purpose, for just before daylight next morning Ah Wee peacefully breathed his last. After breakfast Jim had a strong box constructed in which to transport the body, by pack mule, to Lundy for interment—occasionally throughout the forenoon looking in upon the corpse to see if he could discover any signs of returning animation. So things stood until noon (last Saturday), when Louis Amiot's pack train from this place arrived. The body was then placed in the box and the burden strapped on the back of a pack mule. On reaching the lofty and nearly level ridge, known as Mount Warren divide, Louis hurried up his mules. The one with the corpse began to trot, and the "corpse" began to groan. Louis thought at first it was the mule, and still his hat showed a disposition to crawl up on top of his head. He stopped the mule. The groans became more audible. Then Louis' eyeballs crawled out of his cheeks, took a look at his ears and tried to climb under his hat. Ah Wee was alive again. He was brought to town, placed in comfortable quarters and appeared to be convalescing until 11 o'clock Monday forenoon, when a 'Melican physician and an undertaker (among many others) looked in upon him, when Ah Wee turned his face to the wall and died again—this time for keeps. He was buried Tuesday afternoon with imposing ceremonies of the Chinese kind. Jim Toy said he died of a cold. We inquired if it was not a case of pneumonia. "No, no," said Toy, "Him got no money—him allee time gamble—flee week ago him losee two hundled dolla—him got no money."

And though Townsend wrote little for the papers during this period, his cronies kept his name in print. The fatter dailies, such as the *Virginia Evening Chronicle* and the Bodie *Free Press*, occasionally larded their columns with "biographical" sketches such as the following:

James W. E. Townsend has led a remarkable life. From information imparted by him to his friends while he lived on the Comstock, we learn that he was born in Patagonia, his mother, a noble English lady, having been cast ashore after the wreck of her husband's yacht, in which they were making a pleasure cruise around the globe. She was the only person saved. After the birth of her son, and September having arrived—there being an r in that month—she was killed and eaten. Jim was saved out as a small stake and was played until his twelfth year against the best grub at command of the savage tribe for fattening purposes. Then he escaped on a log, which he paddled through the Straits of Magellan with his hands, and was picked up by a whaler and taken to New Bedford.

At the age of 18 he entered the Methodist ministry and preached with glorious results for ten years, when he went to the Sandwich Islands as a missionary to the Kanaka heathen, and remained for twenty years. Then he reformed and returned to New York and opened a saloon, which for twenty-five years he ran successfully and made a large fortune. In an evil hour for himself, but to the world's advantage, he tried his hand at journalism. Fifteen years of this reduced him once more to poverty and preaching. For thirty years longer Mr. Townsend occupied the pulpit, when he went back again to the saloon business, and after eighteen years of industrious drinking on the part of the public, he brought his wealth to the Pacific Coast. This was in 1849. For several years Mr. Townsend ran simultaneously eight saloons, five newspapers and an immense cattle ranch in various parts of the Golden State.

In 1865 the enterprising gentleman was suddenly afflicted with a disease which for many months compelled him to lie on his back in one position. This misfortune was, with the cruel levity of those rough days, turned to account by his acquaintances, who dubbed him "Lying Jim Townsend," and ever since the sobriquet has stuck to him. For the last decade he has devoted himself exclusively to journalism, and is, of course, once more poor. Some of his friends, who are of a mathematical turn, have, from data furnished them by Mr. Townsend in various conversations, ascertained the remarkable fact that he is 384 years old. Notwithstanding his great age, however, the gentleman still writes with all the vigor of youth, and his shrewd humor is making the *Gazette* more than a local reputation.

When less space was demanded, Townsend's peers ran short fillers which were kicked about from one paper to another: "It is reported that Mr. Jim Townsend has fallen heir to a fortune of £1,000,000, left him by his uncle, Sir Lyon Jem Townsend, who died recently on the Isle of Wight at the extreme age of 119 years."

Ed Cleveland quickly scooped up this spoof and embellished it for the *Free Press*. "Late news confirms this report. On Monday Mr. Townsend will sail for Europe. He writes to the FREE PRESS that upon his return to California he will establish a newspaper in every county in the State and will pay printers $42 per week or $6 per day, five hours to constitute a day's labor. He will also establish a home for Pioneers and a house of refuge for temperance people. It is his intention to conduct an eight-page paper in Bodie, six editions daily, with a chartered saloon for the compositors and editors."

John Ginn also kept his Lundy readers posted on every turn of Jim's fortune, announcing later "Jim Townsend Ruined."

The great fortune which Jim Townsend claims is just within his grasp, as a royalty upon his flying machine invention may yet be lost unless he bestirs himself. A Frenchman is said to have recently invented a balloon-like machine that can be navigated in the air as easily as a boat in water. We cannot believe that any man in the world but Jim is capable of solving the problem of navigating the air. If this Frenchman has a successful machine it is the result of Jim's ideas, of which he has in some way become possessed.

But Jim's greatest boosters were in Virginia City, and thus whenever he could scrape together the change he would hop the

Virginia & Truckee up the grade to the Comstock. There he was always assured of a grand reception by a horde of old friends, a sample of which is recounted by the *Virginia Chronicle* reporter.

Mr. James W. E. Townsend—"Jim," as every body calls him—came up from Reno on Saturday, arriving on the evening train. He was met at the depot by a large delegation of citizens, representing the mining, commercial, newspaper and other industries.

"How are you, Mr. Townsend?" inquired Colonel Boyle, of the Alta mine, grasping the distinguished visitor's hand as he stepped from the car. "We heard you were lame."

"So I am," replied Mr. Townsend, "but I left my limp at Reno. I'll pick it up when I go back."

"You got hurt while out on a hunt, I'm told," remarked Mr. Egan of the Andes mine.

"Yes, but that wasn't the worst of it. A rain storm left us soaking wet, and when I got home I was as stiff as if I had been fed on starch for a year."

"You don't say so," said Mr. Egan.

"Fact, sir, I assure you. I was so stiff they had to take my backbone out to get me to bed."

"When did you leave Bodie, Mr. Townsend?" inquired lawyer Woodburn, as the procession moved up from the depot.

"Left there about ten days ago," replied the great American traveler. "Never saw so much snow in all my life as we had there the past Winter. You couldn't go anywhere without snowshoes."

"You don't say so," said Mr. Woodburn.

"Fact, sir, I assure you. Why we used to have to put on snowshoes even to go to bed. The altitude of that country, you know, is much greater than that of this section. Now, that hill over there," Mr. T. continued, pointing to Cedar Hill, "looks as if it would be hard to climb, doesn't it?"

"It looks so, and it *is* a hard hill to climb," interjected Marshal Corbett.

"Well, gentlemen, that hill's a racetrack compared to some of those in Mono county."

"You don't say so," said Mr. Michael Kelleher, of the California mine.

"Fact, sir, I assure you. Why there's a hill over there near Lundy that they've run a tunnel three hundred feet into, and there isn't room enough on the dump to turn a wheelbarrow in. Steep? I should say it is steep. Why they dropped a car off the dump one day, and it fell two thousand feet before it struck anything; then it bounced off and dropped three thousand feet farther."

"You don't say," reiterated the astonished Mr. Kelleher.

"Fact, sir, I assure you," responded Mr. Townsend, "why, it takes a whole family to look up to the top of that hill."

"They tell me the soil is very fertile down in that Mono Country," said Mr. Ritchie, the barber, who with his German assistant had joined the party.

"Fertile? Well, you'd think so if you saw the way vegetables climb out of the earth half an hour after the snow gets off. It is the most fertile place under the sun—you can raise anything there."

"You don't say so?" said the assistant.

"It's the cold truth sir," said Mr. Townsend. "Why if you only stick a hen's feather into the ground down there in April, it'll grow into a spring chicken by the middle of May."

The assistant staggered into Billy Eckhoff's and called for a stiff "gless ofe schnapps."

"How is the fishing now at Lake Lundy?" asked Mr. Egan.

"Finest you ever saw," replied the great *raconteur.* "Lake's full of splendid trout—gamiest fish in the world, too. They're regular bull dogs, I tell you. Why, they'll climb up your line sometimes and slide down the pole and fight you."

"You don't say so," said Messrs. Egan and Woodburn, in joint astonishment.

"Fact, sir, I assure you. Sometimes they'll come out of the water and chase you along the road and holler for the hook."

"You are somewhat hard of hearing yet, I see, Mr. Townsend," remarked Dr. Webber.

"Yes," replied Mr. T. with a touch of sadness in his voice; "that is the only trouble I have in life. But a man's got to whisper it very low when he says 'Beer' to me on a warm day."

They all went to Billy Schaum's Fredericksburg brewery and unloaded a small fleet of schooners after which the walk and conversation were resumed.

"Why don't you try an ear-trumpet?" asked the Doctor.

"Have tried one—tried whole rafts of 'em. Never saw but one that was of any use to me. That belonged to the young Spaniard who sold the Alexander mine at Grantsville for half a million dollars. He had an ear-trumpet that was shaped like a bar-tumbler, and with that machine clapped to my ear I could hear a man think a mile away."

Dr. Webber said he had to make a professional call, and he left the party rather hurriedly.

Mr. Townsend presently excused himself to the party, as he had to go in search of Matt Riehm, foreman of the Fulton foundry, to see about getting estimates for a cheap ore-crusher which he had recently invented. Speaking of the rapid progress of mechanical invention, he confidentially informed Mr. Surveyor Golding of his profound conviction that, "inside of five years, sir, you'll see a forty-horse-power engine that a man can pack around in his vest pocket."

Mr. Golding raised his hat in respectful admiration, and the dazzled Mr. Townsend went off to the south towns-end, where the Fulton foundry is located. He says he will return to Reno tomorrow morning, as the people down there miss him dreadfully.

TOWNSEND was so overcome by his continued good reception in Virginia City that he at last decided to treat the town to his presence year round, and early in 1885 he left Reno to move up on Sun Mountain. There he indulged in an open-ended cocktail hour at the expense of his more solvent friends. In return, Jim shared with them the tales of his wondrous exploits including his encounter with the "marvelous time piece of Madras." And as more tangible but no less specious evidence of his adventures, he exposed to quick glimpses a reddish rock about the size of a marble, which, in a whisper, he claimed to have plucked with his own hand from the forehead of a great Buddhist idol in the sacred city of Candahar, Afghanistan, during the reign of the mighty Genghis Khan.

Among Jim's drinking companions were Col. Henry Shaw and Alf Doten, respectively the managing and local editors of the *Territorial Enterprise,* and whenever Jim could drink the former under the table he got to "fill in" for him at full managing editor's pay. This made their drinking bouts doubly enjoyable, and Townsend managed to see that the Colonel spreed at least once or twice a week.

In the fall of 1886 Shaw had a brief falling out with Doten, whom he laid off, and on the first of October he appointed Townsend both local and news editor at a pay of thirty dollars a week. Jim held the position on the *Enterprise* for slightly over a month, during which time he found that the rush of business and politics on a daily newspaper gave him little time to invent news. But he did find time to get off a brief item on one of his pet subjects—old Boreas.

The old Washoe zephyr had full swing yesterday and literally owned the town. It was nip-and-tuck with the frisky individual who dared to venture from his place of retreat whether he would ever reach his place of destination or be hurled into the canyon beyond and be buried there beneath the tailings of some defunct old mill. But still the wind kept up. Chimneys were blown down, tin cans, barrels and dogs of all descriptions were hurled promiscuously through the air.

During his month on the *Enterprise,* however, Townsend had more important things to do than fancy-up the weather report. Shaw may have hired him in lingering memory of the Grass Valley incident and Jim's political virtuosity there. Townsend used his new power as editor to renovate and modernize the old paper, and his first act was to push the Republican state and county ticket and platform from its prominent front page position clear onto the back—in the last month before the election. Immediately after the election, Townsend retired from the paper with enough money to buy the *Carson Daily Index* and become its editor and publisher.

The *Carson Daily Index* was born on Christmas day of 1880, the issue of Marshall Robinson, who hoped to profit from the bitter rivalry between Sam Davis's Carson City *Daily Appeal* and Deacon Parkinson's *Nevada Tribune*. Some fifteen years earlier, Robinson had founded the *Daily Appeal*, but lost it during one of its stormy periods. Thus, with no misgivings, he had written in the *Index*'s opening number:

Financially, we are not a bonanza; and commercially we acknowledge ourself a proper subject for the grand bounce. Our diurnal comfort is principally derived from our knowledge that a good many of the people of Nevada are fixed up about as we are. We know of no good reason to fear for the success of our venture. The times couldn't be worse or harder, nor the people much more impoverished. Everything is to be won, and there is nothing more to be lost. We can't lose much on advertisements, for we have started publication without any. We can't lose any money, for the reason that none has been paid to us. It must be apparent, therefore, that the *Index* is planted upon the bedrock foundation of public esteem, and its future consequently secure.

With nothing to lose, the paper did indeed prosper, winning many subscribers and advertisers from its petulant competitors. About 1885 Robinson sold the *Index* to Wells Drury and again retired from the journalistic arena at Carson, but this time more profitably. Drury ran the paper until November 7, 1886, when "other duties" claimed his "undivided attention" and he sold out to Jim Townsend.

Jim offered no salutatory but simply raised his name to the masthead and packed the front page with his usual catch of local items. But as in Virginia City, there was enough real news to leave little time or space for literary excursions of his own, and he soon decided that running a daily was too much work. Still he tried to offer some colorful fare at least once a week, and for the Christmas day issue he treated his readers to "A Queer Experience."

On Wednesday two prospectors met with a very singular experience not far from Steamboat Springs, where they have been sinking a shaft to strike a ledge supposed to be the continuation of that found in Governor Stevenson's Willow Creek mine. They had fired a round of holes in the bottom of the shaft and one of them went down to send up the broken rock while the other remained on top to hoist with the windlass. Pretty soon the latter heard his partner laughing immoderately and could not make out what had got into him. After a few minutes he hailed him:

"What in thunder's the matter with you? I don't see anything funny about shoveling rock into a tub."

He got no answer but the hilarious laughter was kept up as if the fellow down below would burst his suspenders. The top man got angry at the foolishness and went down the ladder to see "what was the matter with the darned fool." He had been down there but a minute or two when a friend came along to the shaft and heard the pair of them shrieking with the wildest kind of laughter, as he said, "just a-raisin' merry hell down there." So he went down to join in the fun, and pretty soon he, too, began to bubble with hilarity, and all three howled in unison, but the last comer, being of a scientific turn, dropped upon the cause of the excessive cachinnation. They had struck a vent of protoxide of nitrogen, which is laughing-gas—not an unusual thing in that vicinity, but it is seldom found in such volume as to affect a person to such an extent as they experienced.

But Townsend was eager to sell the newspaper and move on, for the work of putting out a daily was too hard and the prospects too dim. Late in 1886 Carson City was awash in newspapers, having four dailies and one weekly struggling to win a sustaining share of the patronage of less than a thousand possible subscribers and a handful of advertisers. Thus Townsend must have felt shrewd when he unloaded the paper on January 26, 1887, after less than three months of ownership.

11

A Hole in the Ground

S TEADILY DECLINING silver prices in the early 1880s were pushing the mining industry into a depression destined to close down many mines throughout the west. Mono County was especially hard hit with most of its mines shutting down before the end of 1884. The bulk of the mining operations around Lundy were in the hands of two companies, the May Lundy Mining Company in Lake Canyon and the Great Sierra Consolidated Mining Company on Tioga Hill. They provided the economic foundation for the town, and their collapse that summer caused the virtual abandonment of Lundy.

As a herald of impending hard times, John Ginn had started the year with a campaign to retrieve outstanding bills by the weekly publication of such blackmailing duns as:

O. SEIM (OF BODIE)
STAND UP HERE !

You needn't be scared—we're not going to give you away. In fact, it was only our sense of fairness that caused us to call you up at all—because we have so many other and more unconscionable frauds to deal with. But in looking over our *old* book— the one we filled and closed two years ago—our senses reeled at the multiplicity of delinquents there written down, and as we desired to treat them all fairly, we borrowed Maestretti's jury box, wrote the name of each delinquent upon a slip of paper, placed them all in the box, shook them up and drew— O. Seim! We were sorry that it came that way, for we didn't want to make the fact public that when you resigned the foremanship of the Homer mine you subscribed for the INDEX and had it sent to you at No. 23 Alta street, San Francisco, from January 16, 1882, until the next November, or until you left there to go to work in the Bodie Tunnel, that you never paid for the paper, and that although we sent the bill and wrote to you several times when we learned that you were working in the Bodie Tunnel, we have never heard a word from you—all this we regret to make public, and are also sorry to keep the multitude, whose names are still in the jury box, waiting for their medicine. However, if you will send us the $5 you owe us we will leave your name out of the brief but expressive black list to which we intend to relegate the name of each fraud as soon as we "stand him up" so that the public can spot, and thereafter avoid, him—and which black list, by the way (as soon as we get a good "starter" for it), we intend to publish weekly until we change the INDEX to a daily, and daily thereafter till the mines of Mill Creek are worked down to the 300-foot level.

(P. S.—There'll be another drawing next week.)

Perhaps an intimidated few shuffled forward to square their debts before their turn came to stand up, but the great majority held out, and Ginn's blacklist darkened rapidly over the following months. He soon learned, too, that he was not alone in being unable to collect his due. For in July the Great Sierra Consolidated Mining Company was forced to close down from failure of its stockholders to pay an assessment, and four weeks later the sheriff shut down the May Lundy mines and mill under attachment of roughly forty thousand dollars due local merchants and miners. Rumors floated that the May Lundy property was merely in the process of being sold to new owners who would resume operations in a few days. With this slim hope Ginn continued the paper from week to week, writing cheering little items about what lively times they would all be having in just a few days when the mining company paid up and work started up again.

After two and a half months, however, even Ginn realized that this day would be a cold one. On November 1, 1884, he issued his last number of the *Index* without any valedictory or notice of suspension—just as though it were still to continue. And with the type still standing in the forms from that issue, he locked up the office and took the stage down the canyon to Hawthorne, where he boarded a train for Oakland.

Ginn edited the Oakland *Tribune* for barely a month and then moved on east to El Paso, Texas. But the *Homer Mining Index* office remained closed, and inside the dust settled on the standing type, the ink dried in the bottles, the roller began to crack and warp, and the floor sagged beneath the weight of the press and cases. The walls and roof were pierced by winds, rain, and snow to scatter, soak, and mildew the unused paper, to freeze and crack the imposing stone and to rot and twist the frames. In the summer of 1886 the office came near cremation when a fire raged through the abandoned buildings in the lower half of town. To all appearances the *Homer Mining Index* was dead.

Bodie, too, was badly hit by foreclosures and suspensions which within two years had closed over forty mines, leaving just five running by the end of 1884. Cleveland and Osborne of the Bodie *Free Press* sought a new spring climate early in 1884, and in August they purchased the Los Angeles *Evening Express*. The *Free Press* was leased to H. L. Childs, the new public land commissioner, upon whose advertising the paper had been almost wholly dependent. But Childs was unable to make the paper pay, and the following year he joined John Ginn in Sonora, turning the *Free Press* over to James Parker, in whose hands it died on July 9, 1886.

Dan Jones's Bodie *Evening Miner* thus became the camp's surviving newspaper. But even with a monopoly on the printing, Jones was soon forced to reduce the *Miner* to a weekly, supported mostly by delinquent stock assessment notices, which made up over two-thirds of his paying advertisements.

Dan's remaining rival in the county was the antiquated Bridgeport *Chronicle-Union*, published at the county seat by Alex and Bob Folger. The Folger brothers had sewed up the county legal advertising and printing through what Jones alleged to be the lowest and most despicable conniving and were running their paper on the publication of the delinquent tax rolls. Dan had been waging a mild journalistic war with the Folgers since the inception of the *Miner*, and when they became his sole combatants, Jones fought with vigor. But it proved to be a long war of attrition, for both were well accustomed to surviving on the thin broth which the economy of the county afforded. Nonetheless the ensuing invective provided the only vitality to the otherwise lifeless columns of both papers.

Bob Folger was quick to attack Jones for his occasional intemperance, and every time the *Miner* would miss an issue, Folger would immediately announce that the paper was now "dead as a herring." This went on for nearly two years, and when Jones at last showed signs of capitulation by advertising the *Miner* for sale, Folger leaped into print with a lengthy obituary for him the following week. To this Dan blasted back: "Now I am astounded, although I had promised myself that I would never again be surprised at any low piece of dirty villainy which R. M. & A. C. Folger might perpetrate. For four long weary years those two unprincipled things have studied and labored, night and day, to concoct some plan whereby they could get Orlando E. Jones out of Mono County. Plots have they laid; inductions deep, dangerous, and damnable, to accomplish this end—the only end in life for which these two things seem now to live. I cannot call them men, for they are merely things, and very useless things at that." Thus the journalistic rivalry in this moribund county continued in an unending exchange, futile blow for futile blow.

BUT EVEN before the actual suspension of the May Lundy mines, George Washington Butterfield, one of the part-owners, decided to make good use of the already confused litigation over the title of the mines. In May of 1884 he had sailed for London to try to float a new stock company to work the mines, to which he unblushingly claimed a full and clear title. He had first organized the West May Lundy Company, Ltd., which was to raise a capital of $5,000,000 to purchase and work the "twenty-three mines" he claimed as his and which he agreed to sell the company for a trifling $4,500,000 in cash and stock. But aside from the May Lundy, a working mine worth an estimated $200,000, all the other "mines" were undeveloped locations of only prospective value. When word of the scheme reached San Francisco, Frederick Marriott of the *News-Letter* was the first to point up the fraudulence of the venture, commenting, "Five million dollars for a lot of locations of mines, as many of them are jocosely termed, is one of the richest jokes we have heard for many a day. Some people are apt nowadays to call a hole in the ground a mine."

These remarks were picked up by the London papers and under the blast of such bad press, Butterfield sought to cover his tracks by changing the name of the venture to the Homer District Consolidated Gold Mines Ltd. This change fooled no one, however, and the *News-Letter* fired another salvo, noting that the "fraudulent attempt to carry out the project under the name of May Lundy" was now being "reproduced with a devilish cunning" under a new one. Further adding that "the unparalleled audacity of the persons who concocted this outrageous scheme deserves the most scathing criticism," Marriott rolled out a detailed expose of the fraud. The expose was carried in London by the *Financial News*, which also advised those who had already signed up for stock in the company not to pay in on it and to get out.

As other papers joined in the denunciation of the fraud, Butterfield was beset from all sides, and a lesser man might have admitted capture. But Butterfield, still the undaunted opportunist, set about to fish other profit from the torrent of accusations swirling about him. Hoping to double his profit, he slapped a libel suit on the London *Financial News* for $5,000,000 in damages. A partial settlement from this alone would pay him well for his efforts, even if he never sold another scrap of stock.

All Butterfield needed to win the case was to prove the worth of the Lundy mines, and thus in late September of 1888 he returned to Lundy for a few weeks to arrange for more "expert" appraisals of the mines. Convinced that he could offer no better proof of their value than the continued praise of a local press, he quickly set about making arrangements to revive the *Homer Mining Index* to give both the mines and the town the appearance of activity and prosperity. And what better choice could he have made for editor than "Lying Jim" Townsend?

12

Resurrection

W HEN JIM TOWNSEND returned to Lundy Canyon in the fall of 1888, he found the town nearly abandoned. The principal mines had been closed for over four years, and there were scarcely three dozen miners scattered throughout the entire district. In the town itself only a fraction of the original structures still stood—the fire two years before had completely destroyed the lower half of the town, and heavy winter snows had felled all but the sturdiest buildings remaining. Of those, less than two dozen were occupied. But Jim had conducted lively newspapers in virtually lifeless communities before, and an actually defunct Lundy only added to the challenge.

The *Index* office was still standing, but its interior was "pied from Genesis to Revelations," and Townsend spent several weeks putting it back into running order. Finally he got the old press working again with one broken leg propped on a Bible. Using home-brewed rollers of the Dan Jones recipe, he resurrected the *Homer Mining Index* on October 13. Since John Ginn had left all of the type standing from his last issue, four years before, the task of reviving the paper was greatly simplified. Townsend simply lifted his name to the masthead, advanced the date and serial number, and freshened up the news and local items inside. Leaving all the old advertisements still running, he unveiled a very healthy and prosperous looking corpse of a paper. Nearly all the numbers of each issue were bundled up and sent to Butterfield in London, where they were circulated among his actual and prospective stockholders. The remainder were sent as exchanges to the Nevada and San Francisco papers and to Jim's friends.

It was such a good joke that Townsend felt compelled to share it with all his old cronies, but when he wrote Sam Davis of the Carson *Appeal* to brag that he was "running a newspaper that hasn't a live advertisement and does not boast a single subscriber" the whole ruse came near being exposed. For Sam decided to spread the joke through his columns, where it was picked up and copied by the Reno *Gazette* and the Virginia City papers. Fortunately it seems to have slipped the notice of Fred Marriott of the San Francisco *News-Letter*, and thus Jim's London readers were not yet let in on the joke.

Eventually Townsend ran only live local ads and actually gained a few paying subscribers, but he still had to fill out the columns with outdated mining patent notices and leftover patent medicine ads. But his main purpose was to provide good press for the moribund May Lundy property by portraying it as an active and paying mine—the mainstay of a prosperous mining camp. To achieve this he commenced a series of weekly mining reports that read like none other ever written. While legitimate reports would list in detail the number of men employed, the number of feet run on a particular drift or crosscut, and the tonnage of rock and ore removed, Jim spoke only in relatives, generalities, and vague but promising superlatives, a fine example of which read:

Work at the May Lundy mine is progressing about the same as usual, therefore there is nothing new to report, but we cannot help remarking that three times the present force ought to be employed. There is ore enough in the mine to keep in constant operation a much larger mill than that now in use, and if the managers were endowed with true business instincts, they would be able to see what they were missing.

And for good measure he could not help adding: "It seems to us that they scrupulously avoid trying to make money out of the mine."

For actual news, however, Townsend became more specific, if not more convincing, in his local items, which he ran up under the heading "JOTS AND SPLINTERS: Facts and Fancies of Local Interest."

J. W. Heilshorn, President of the Dead Broke Mining Company, and William Monahan, Superintendent of the Consolidated Trout Sluicers of Busted Flat, are in town.

They say that Nick Baule will start a saloon here, so as to catch the mafia trade. That will make eight boozing places. There ought to be about eleven more, so that each working man may have a saloon dependent upon his own personal patronage. Then he could give his monthly check to the saloon man and there would be no bother about making change. We invite everybody to come. There is room for all. A board across two barrels is good enough.

An enterprising individual made a location in Lake Canyon recently, and at one end planted a pole in a snow drift fifty feet deep. The other end he could not get to, but seeing a coyote sitting on a shelf about the right distance off, he took him for the north lode-line monument, which fact he stated in the notice that he posted on the pole. The animal will, of course stay there and see that nobody jumps the claim.

A man named Quinn—or something like it—found a long rope near Mt. Gibbs a while ago, and dragged it all the way to Devil's Canyon, the other side of Hite's Cove, in Mariposa

County, about 70 miles away. When he got home he was astonished to find a horse attached to the east end of it. Being a religious man, and firmly married to a school-marm too, he was stupendously puzzled over the circumstances. The horse belonged to George Troy, who with Harry Branch, followed the trail until it terminated at the Quinn domicile. The truly religious gentleman was dumb-founded and paralyzed, likewise the quondam pedagoguess because young Troy remarked that the abduction of the animal looked very much like horse-stealing, as they view things in Mono. However he was willing to even things up and return the animal, which he did, adding an order on a neighbor for $12.00 to pay for the detective's grub on the way home. Troy was half minded to have the man arrested, but remembering a late experience at law, he concluded to let the matter go as it lay and returned home.

And for filler the weather was always worth an item:

A Screaching Blizzard

The prediction of the Piute Wiggins has been verified. He said a storm would come, and it was on time. A Captain in the Signal Service with a bushel of brass buttons on his coat-front couldn't have done better. A week ago last Thursday—the morning after the picnic and ball—the windy riot began. When the excursionists went down the canyon the wind was blowing at the rate of sixty miles an hour, but it had only begun to slouch along. Charley Hayes was the last man to leave, and he went off with his buggy enveloped in a flame of dust and splinters, as if called to glory. He writes to us that his hind wheels didn't touch the ground for five miles. That little zephyr was only a primer. Next day it put on more steam and Old Boreas worked his bellows with a fiendish vigor until Saturday morning, when he "throwed her wide open and turned her loose." It was a dandy. The snow was blown out so straight that some of it did not strike the ground until it got to Benton. And so we had it until midnight on Tuesday, when it cleared up and became freezing cold. Then we had a rest for a few hours, but the elements continued to spit like cats. Wednesday morning the riot broke out afresh—this time from the east. Whew! How it did shriek and howl and play havoc with everything that wasn't bolted to solid granite. Snow came in impenetrable masses, whirling up one canyon and down another, as if it had lost something. Towards night it let up. The barometers were kicking and bucking like wall-eyed mustangs. Onkst's weather-gauge went up, the INDEX instrument went down, and so made a stand-off, enabling us to hold Boreas level for a while. A few spasmodic efforts followed, but the old fellow couldn't catch his second wind, and everything is lovely again—lovelier than ever.

But when winter finally descended upon the camp, Jim complained,

We have been unable to get out of doors this week, therefore we don't know what transpired on the other side of mountainous snowdrifts that encircle the INDEX office. We have seen the tops of the mountains and the snow-banners flying from them in streaks of silver when the sun broke through the clouds. Tuesday forenoon nothing could be seen six inches from the window. Gusts of wind came with the speed of a cannon-ball, picking up banks of snow and making the air opaque. We have seen nobody and heard nothing. If we had been sealed up in the tank and sunk in the lake we could hardly know less. *But* we give our readers the usual quantity of inspired hogwash.

With the coming of spring, some vitality returned to the camp, and on April 2 the citizens of Lundy held their annual celebration of "Resurrection Day." It was a unique event at which time they called upon everyone for miles around to come and help herald the spring by trampling down the last lingering snow-patches of winter. In March of 1889 Jim ran a much-leaded but full-column ad, announcing:

RESURRECTION:

———

GRAND CELEBRATION AT LUNDY

Seven Thousandth Anniversary
of the 666th. chapter of the
Most Venerable Resurrectionists
of Lundy
TUESDAY . . . APRIL 2, 1889

GABRIEL will Sound his Trumpet at 9 o'clock A.M., in the Dark of the Moon, when Repentant Brothers in Good Standing on the Books of the Recording Angel will present themselves for inspection.

Disengaged Saints from Subordinate Chapters will tune their harps at the first appearance of the Awful Shadow and report to Brother August Cordes, who will remain in seclusion at the Sanctuary to examine Credentials.

The Procession will form at 10 o'clock, and march in the Dark of the Moon to the Bright Side of Venus.

After the Resurrection Ceremonies there will be a Grand Banquet to which all are invited.

In the evening there will be a Grand

RESURRECTION BALL.

At MILLER'S HALL, Mono Lake. All are invited to attend. The best of music and charge.

The following week Townsend recounted the festivities, proclaiming,

Resurrection Day was a jubilee in Mill Creek Canyon and for a radius of ten miles. There was fun from soda to hock, though whisky, washed down with beer, was the chief tipple. Honest miners and wild-eyed ranchers on "unfiery, tamed steeds" swarmed into camp until the sidewalks were jammed with a swarming mass of humanity. There must have been a hundred, counting the gentlemen who lay around in a delirium of forgetfulness.

Gabriel sounded his trumpet early in the lovely morning, and was warmly responded to by many a horn. The procession formed, the right leaning against the brewery, the left hanging onto the bar at the store with both hands. The Lundy brass band led by Professor Ed. Hubbard, played "When Gabriel blows his trumpet early in the morning," and the procession was set in motion by Grand Marshal Campbell, assisted by Louis Amiot.

They marched and counter-marched from store to brewery and from brewery to store, until they wished there was a saloon in the middle. About this time the Grand Marshal missed his tip on the lee lurch and succumbed to internal pressure, and did not again report for duty until next day, when it was noticed that he was badly damaged about the gills. The procession being left without a leader disbanded. Toward evening the Resurrectionists started for Mono Lake, where there was to be a ball at the school house. They had a glorious time until sunrise, when they returned to Lundy in four-horse outfits.

On Wednesday they rested and freshened their nip in a quiet way, but next day the enthusiasm broke out anew, and the camp was in a turmoil of preparation for the crowning glory of the celebration at the Lundy school house that night. It was a high carnival of delirious joy—an eruptive volcano of mirth, and none of the participants will hasten to forget the fun they had. Resurrection Day, 1889, will be a green spot in the memory of all who joined in the festivities.

Real news items were exceedingly rare, however, and Townsend more often complained, "If anybody thinks it is an easy matter to grind out a lot of truck in this wilderness every week, let him come here and try it on, and we'll sit down and watch his head ache, agreeing to keep the stove red hot and the cat's nose out of the soup kettle, which is half the battle." Thus most of his "truck" was gleaned from his fertile brain with the gentle persuasion of whisky.

First he conjured the creatures in Mono Lake, but stranger visions were to follow:

It has been universally believed that no creature of any kind can exist in the waters of Mono Lake; but Judge Mattly explodes this notion. Last Saturday he saw a strange creature flopping about in the shallow water near the shore. The thing seemed to open and shut like spy-glass; at its longest it was about six feet in length and two feet in diameter. It resembled an enormous leech more than anything else, and apparently propelled itself by drawing in air and forcing it out behind. When enflated it was egg-shaped and sat upon the water like a bell-buoy. No flipper or fins of any description were visible, nor anything that resembled a mouth. The orifices through which it evidently inhaled air could not be seen. The Judge described it as a disgusting mass of green pulp.

Then he told a tale of mysteriously missing sheep:

For several years sheepmen have steered clear of Mount Dana, of which they have a superstitious dread. Hundreds of animals would mysteriously disappear, and the most vigilant search failed to develop a trace of them. The strange shortage of mutton is now satisfactorily explained. On the southern slope of the mountain a deep crevasse has been discovered, eight to ten feet in width and several hundred feet long, extending downward to the base of the hill. On the north side of the opening an odd natural accident presents itself. A flat rock about fifty feet square is so evenly balanced that the weight of a few men will cause it to teeter.

A few days ago the Mount Dana mystery was solved: A shepherd's flock had scattered, and while bunching them a band fled to this tilting rock, which cocked up to an angle of forty-five degrees and slid them into the black cavern below. The sudden disappearance of his flock startled the unnaturalized Portuguese, who straightway began to work up a solution to the puzzle. After a long search he found a way into the dark rift, and there were bones, pelts and sheep debris enough to cause a Hudson Bay Frenchman to dream of glory. Hundreds of animals had fallen into it from the tilting rock. There will no longer be any mystery about the disappearance of sheep at Mount Dana.

Then he began to see strange lights on the rocky slope above Lundy Lake, and wrote of "Dancing Boulders" reminiscent of Dan De Quille's "Travelling Stones of Pahranagat."

On the slope of Mount Gilcrest above the lake opposite Lundy a strange light was observed one evening recently. The INDEX man and a companion crossed the lake and ascended to the place where the light was seen, when they witnessed a group of granite boulders, some of them weighing many tons, all trembling violently, as if afflicted with severe ague, while the phosphorescent flashes emitted by them imparted an uncanny effulgence to surrounding objects. A hundred tons of granite boulders shivering like a Shaker prayer meeting and illuminated by a ghost-fire would puzzle anybody. Next morning they returned to the spot, and found the boulders silent and inert, and looking as innocent as any other blocks of granite, but there was abundant evidence that they had been in motion, perhaps at long intervals for ages. They had each ground out an egg-shaped hollow in the bedrock, the long way in every instance being from north to south, and varying in depth from two feet to nine or ten. In the center of the group is a mass of magnetic iron ore. What influence this magnetic mass has upon the surrounding boulders is inexplicable at present, but it may be that by some freak of nature it becomes a storage battery, and when surcharged with the accumulations of years, alternately attracts and repels the adjacent boulders, thus giving them the ague, as it were.

And finally he told the tale of "A Sleep-Walker's Wealth":

One of our most energetic prospectors is in trouble but, contrary to the usual run of things, there is much money in his trouble. We will call him Billy, because it isn't his name. For the past two or three weeks he has been "all broke up," mentally and physically, but not financially, for he is accumulating wealth daily, and this assuages the pain of the puzzle. He is working a wonderfully rich mine, and a startling remark to make—he don't know where his bonanza is, though he is getting $200 to $300 a day out of it. This may seem improbable, but glittering facts are stubborn and convincing.

Two weeks ago last Sunday he awoke in the morning late, stiff sore, and "all broke up," in the profoundest depths of nervous degradation, so to speak. The first thing that attracted his attention was a well-filled canvas sack. He recognized the sack, but how it became filled he couldn't tell. Opening it, he found it contained the richest quartz he ever saw—"two-thirds gold and the rest worth a dollar an ounce," he said. There were fifty or sixty pounds of it, and how it got into his cabin was beyond his comprehension; but thinking that some friend of his had been foraging around the May Lundy dump and uncovered a portion of the treasure said to be hidden there, and had placed it in his cabin during the night for safe keeping, he said nothing about the matter during the day. Next morning he found another sack of ore near his bed. Naturally enough, he was puzzled and at the same time "all broke up," as we have said before.

The following morning there was another sack, and so it continued for a week—fifty or sixty pounds of the richest kind of specimen quartz each day. Not being inclined to fly in the face of Providence, or to turn up his nose at what appeared to be manna from Heaven, he set to work with his hand-mortar and beat out more gold in one day than he had ever possessed before, all the while working in a thick fog of mystery. Day after day he pounded away, and each morning another sack of specimens was deposited in his cabin by unseen hands.

Billy was now in such a state of perturbation over the mystery—such a condition of nervous sensitiveness—that he feared to sleep alone with his rapidly accumulating wealth, and so imparted his secret to Constable McKenzie, who consented to occupy a bunk in his cabin last Wednesday night. They "turned in" about 8 o'clock, as we all do in Lundy, and all went smoothly until midnight, when McKenzie was awakened by Billy's movements in the bunk below. The latter got up and pulled on his trowsers and boots. The moon shining brightly in at the open door, every action was observable. McKenzie did not speak, nor did he think there was anything unusual in his companion's conduct until he saw him leave the house with a pick and an empty sack. Then it flashed through his head that there was something queer in the air, and he speedily donned his clothes and followed.

Mac is as agile as an antelope and tough as a lawyer's conscience, but he could not overtake the fleeing Billy, who was climbing the steepest ridge of Mount Gilcrest, as if being hoisted by supernatural agency. Above the upper fork of the Lake Canyon road he disappeared among the almost inaccessible crags, and Mac gave over the chase, knowing that no ordinary man could follow unless he had the claws of a jaybird and a screw-propeller in the slack of his breeches. So he returned to the cabin and went to bed, wondering.

About 4 o'clock Billy staggered into the house under a heavy load, which he deposited upon the floor, and without ado rolled into his bunk and began to "saw cigar-boxes." Then Mac got up and examined the contents of the sack Billy had brought. "The same old stuff," he said to himself. "Ten dollars a pound, sure."

About 7 o'clock Billy got up, and was unmistakably astonished to find another sack of rich ore at hand. Meantime Mac had solved the problem. His companion was a somnambulist. By delicate approaches, he gradually broached the matter, when Billy confessed that he had often been detected in sleep walking, but knew nothing of what occurred during the somnolent periods. He had for some years been trying to find the Lost Top-Sawyer and had over taxed his mind with the idea, so that his brain was actively at work on it when he was asleep. He has no recollection of having left his cabin any night, but the gold in hand—nearly $4,000—proves that he has been somewhere. He has consented to be closely watched at night by two friends, so that he may be traced to his bonanza. From the direction he takes and the quartz he gets, it is presumed that the sleep-walker has re-discovered the Lost Top-Sawyer.

These tall tales were eagerly copied by Townsend's California and Nevada exchanges, a number of which, such as the Carson *Morning Appeal*, the Virginia City *Evening Chronicle* and the Sonora *Tuolumne Independent*, carried a weekly digest of quips and items from the *Index* running to as much as two columns.

Of course these endeavors did not make Jim's pronouncements on the worth of the May Lundy property any more believable in London. And his reputation suffered even more in the summer of 1889 when Sam Davis wrote a satirical sketch for the Sunday supplement of the San Francisco *Examiner*, entitled "My Friend the Editor." With thinly disguised allusion to Townsend and the *Homer Mining Index*, Davis described a fictitious paper, the *Manganetus Index*, whose editor was quoted as saying:

There is a group of mines near here which certain capitalists of San Francisco are anxious to place upon the London market. They have hired me to advocate these mines, and it is part of my bargain to run my paper in such a way that the London readers will think that a large town is flourishing in the mountains.

My imagination is not sluggish, and so I manufacture all I write. I leave no stone unturned to make the mythical city of Manganetus a live, bustling town. You will find in this issue a public meeting called to discuss the question of a new bridge across a stream that exists only in the columns of the *Index*. Here is the wife of a prominent mining superintendent eloping with a member of the City Council; here is a runaway team, knocking the smithereens out of a cigar-store. You will note the advertisement of the cigar-store in another column. Here is the killing of "Texas Pete" and the investigation of his death by a Coroner's jury. The cause of the shooting was a dispute relative to the ownership of a mining location of fabulous richness. There is also in another portion of the paper, a legal summons advertised calling on a co-owner (one of the principals in the affray) to do his assessment work or lose his interest. All my work dovetails nicely in, has a plausible look and shows no flaw, yet it is all absolutely made from whole cloth.

This, doubtless, was the final coup to Butterfield's scheme, and by fall suits were brought against the company in London. Butterfield's libel action against the *Financial News* was also about to be quashed. But in one last futile effort to save his scheme, he had obtained court permission to have a hearing held at the British Consulate in San Francisco to present the testimony of mining experts as to the worth of the May Lundy. One of his principal witnesses was to be that noted mining expert J. W. E. Townsend.

13

The Talking Machine of Lundy

IN LATE October of 1889, Jim Townsend left Lundy for San Francisco to give his testimony at the British Consulate on Butterfield's behalf. In jovial spirits and with customary accuracy, he informed his friends that he was taking a five-week trip to London—evidently on one of his "flying machines." He left the *Index* temporarily in the hands of Ferd Frost, who circulated wild rumors of Townsend's exploits during his absence. Frost predicted that Jim would be warmly received all along his route and commented: "We expect to hear of Mr. Townsend in the newspapers published in the towns through which he will have to pass with articles headed something like the following: 'Lieing Jim Is In Town;' 'Truthful James Is Among Us;' 'Christ Has Come;' 'The Prevaricator of the *Homer Index* Taking in the

Sights;' 'The Talking Machine of Lundy Has Arrived and Will
Deliver a Temperance Lecture to a Select Few.'"

But even before Frost wrote these lines Jim had descended
upon Carson City, and Sam Davis proclaimed:

JIM   TOWNSEND   IN   CARSON !
He Has a Pocket Full of Rocks, and Paints the City.

Yesterday morning the editor of the APPEAL was passing
Thompson's restaurant, when suddenly he was aware of a
strong hand grasping his coat collar, and a moment later he was
whisked into the restaurant by an irresistible force.

"Hullo, you old —— —— ——, bless my regenerate soul;
how are you?"

It was at once apparent to the editorial mind that the writer
had fallen into the clutches of Jim Townsend, editor of the *Homer Mining Index*, otherwise known as the "Mono County
Snowslide." It was the same old Jim that left Carson three years
ago and he had not changed a hair. His old familiar salutation,
with him a term of endearment, came out with the old fog horn
accents.

"Sit down," he shouted; "and help me paralyze the clams.
Don't care if you have had breakfast; sit down I say;" and he
downed the writer with a powerful jerk.

"I say, waiter, bring on two dozen on the half-shell, two dozen
of those clams; call 'em oysters do ye? So long since I saw any
I've forgotten the name. You can't tell what they are after I get
my molar stamps droppin' on 'em. Hy there, I say some tender-
loin steak, two virgin pullets on toast and a quart bottle of Ro-
de-rio."

The waiter began to move round, but not quite fast enough
for James and he called him back.

"Here my boy, you must skip with considerable alacrity. I've
got a Mill Creek appetite, and here's Mill Creek bullion to pay
for it."

He took out a large sack and began to thump the table with
it.

"I don't hit civilization often. Why old boy, only last Friday
night I had to go to bed on snow shoes.

"That's right, chuck those clams—oysters I mean, down lively, and I'll shout for more. I say waiter, two dozen more oysters, and set the kid at work openin' more. Remember you're feedin' three years of starvation on Mill Creek.

"Hot out there in the Summer, do you say? Well rather; last 4th of July I had to keep ice in my mouth all day to keep my teeth from sweating.

"Say, waiter, put another bottle on ice and see that when you paste the label on that it's the right one.

"Hey there, come back; if that was Charlie Thompson who just passed, go out and snake him in. Haven't eaten with Charlie for years."

The waiter rushed out and soon returned with Thompson.

"Sit down, you old — — —, and help us eat. Get out some more bivalves and husk the shell off the top side of the varmints and poke the stove under 'em.

"Sit down Charlie; waiter, another bot. How do I feel? Finer 'n a cut off shot gun.

"Here fasten your grinders into that maiden pullet and fill up your glass.

"Book keeping much now Charlie? Well my Uncle Mose, killed in the siege of Lucknow, was a lightning striker at figures. I've seen him stumble over a tomb stone on a dark night blind drunk and in the morning when he got up, tell you the weight of the corpse when it died. He'd figure up nine columns — —, waiter more oysters, dozen all round and get some more on deck for we're still a comin'.

"What these fellows don't get away with, I'll take myself, we want something to stay our stomachs until dinner time.

"Which way? I'm off for London tonight and I'm heeled with the scads. I'll take some chunks of gold specimens there that'll make Victoria want some shares of the mine.

"Mining, d'ye call it? Stop right there, don't ever talk of mining in Lundy, it's quarrying, we take the metal out in blocks.

"Have you those other three dozen oysters ready waiter? We don't want to wait all the morning for oysters. Keep cooking and keep bringin', run till we holler quit.

"Smother those trout in cream when you bake 'em and get the half shells in here lively.

"What, not use cream in Lundy? I have cream all the year round, you get butter from Sacramento, chuck it into a churn and run it backwards a spell; you run it right back into cream. See?"

After about twelve dozen oysters had been disposed of, Townsend began to show signs of abating his onslaught on the meal and said briefly,

"'Nuff oysters."

"Here is the beef steak and the fish you ordered," said the waiter, bringing it in.

"Just chuck the fish back into the wagon and salt the meat down till I get back from London," said Jim as he settled the score and started up the street.

Thus fed, Townsend struck out for his hotel where he polished up his mining expertise on some of the patrons. Sam Davis tagged along to hear the sport, which he later served up to his readers. Jim started the conversation by remarking,

"If you want to see mining on a big scale go to Mono county."

"How big?" said a little man close by.

"Why, the Big Hole Mine, that I am connected with, has the deepest shaft and the biggest workings in the world."

"How deep?" said the little man.

"You can't measure it, because if we stopped work long enough to see how deep the shaft was, it would materially interfere with the bullion product. We dropped a line down once and reeled it out until it broke with his own weight. When a boy falls down the shaft, he strikes the bottom a grandfather."

"Must have a big pay roll."

"We used to send the money down to the hands in cages until the workings got so deep that we didn't get the winter account settled until a way along in the spring. So we started a bank and telegraphed the money orders. That system saved us an awful wear and tear on the cages. The miners live down there and rear their families. They got an underground city bigger 'n Carson, with a regular charter and municipal elections twice a year. They publish two daily papers and a literary magazine."

"I never heard of the magazine," said the stranger.

"Of course not, it would be a year old when it got to you. Besides they hold a fair there annually and racing every Saturday. Finest four mile track in the world, lit with electric light. No mud, no dust, always in the same condition. Perfect paradise for sports. What do you think of that for a mine?"

Here the stranger, who was a Californian, threw his leg carelessly over the arm of a chair, and lighting a cigar, replied in a deep earnest tone:

"I don't think much of your mine. You work too much for small results. When your mine plays out you have a lot of old truck on your hands, and where are you? You mine after primitive methods, like all new countries. It takes experience and head work to tackle the industry in a proper shape. With your mine you must be on the ground in person, and have any amount of men to look after this department or that. Now I have a bigger mine than yours, it is located in Storey county, somewhere in the northern part, I believe, and I run it quite up to the handle with one or two assistants."

"How deep might the shaft be?"

"It might be pretty deep if I allowed the men to rush forward and overdo the thing, but at present there is no shaft at all."

"Hoisting works up?"

"No, no hoisting works—not if I know it. You can fool away a great deal of good hard coin on hoisting works."

"How in thunder do you run your mine?"

"On the assessment plan, sir. That's the latest and most improved method. We have a big map of the mine hung up in the company's office, made by one of the most competent artists on the Coast. Now when we have a good map of the lower working we don't need any works to speak of. We photograph the Savage hoisting works from the top of the Hale & Norcross trestleworks—an entirely new view—and call it by our name; the Bullion Brick. I keep a man in Virginia at $60 a month to super-

intend the location and write weekly letters, and I stay in San
Francisco in my office on Pine Street and levy the assessments
every 60 days; that's as often as the law allows. I'm the president, board of trustees, secretary, treasurer, and everything—
more especially the treasurer. Of course, I draw the salary for
all the officers, and when I get through drawing salaries I turn
the rest over to the agent in Virginia to pay off the hands. By
not employing any hands he saves enough to pay himself. My
regular income from the mine is $200,000 a year, and never a
pick stuck in the ground. This is what I consider scientific mining, sir. You get the silver out of the pockets of the stockholders
and leave the vast argentiferous and auriferous deposits in your
claim for your children, who can go right ahead and develop
the mine just as soon as the people quit putting up, which isn't
at all likely to occur. As soon as a man drops on the game he
dies, and the new comers have to learn for themselves. As long
as people are being born in Nevada and California, my mine
will run on like a chronometer clock."

"But," said Jim, "my style of mining keeps a lot of men at
work."

"So does mine," quoth the Golden Gate Chap. "Thousands
of men are working night and day to pay the assessments. It
keeps the country as busy as a beehive," and the speaker sauntered to the telegraph office to order assessment No. 36.

TOWNSEND arrived in San Francisco early the following week
and immediately checked in at the Palace. When the desk clerk
handed him the registration book, he turned it sideways and
with a flourish scrawled his name across the whole page. The
clerk glowered back and then counted up the number of lines
taken by Jim's signature and informed him that he owed for eighteen persons beside himself. Townsend winced in explanation
that "John Hancock once wrote his name on a piece of paper
much larger than that and nothing was said about it." But the
clerk was unmoved, and Jim retired with a bankrupted look to
his room.

Later that evening he set out to do the town, and about two
o'clock in the morning, so the story goes, he wandered into a

saloon on the Embarcadero. Introducing himself as Captain Townsend, he invited everyone to take a drink with him, after which he regaled them for an hour with sea stories. Impressed, a shanghaier slipped Jim a spiked drink, putting him fast asleep by the time the saloon closed. He was lowered into a boat and rowed to a ship at anchor in the bay. But after he awoke in the afternoon his utter incompetency as a sailor caused him to be quickly fired ashore.

Townsend had been beaten at nearly every turn on this trip, and the situation was not to change the following week with the commencement of the hearing on the May Lundy mines at the British Consulate. Underestimating the extent of the prosecution's information, Townsend testified that he had been a practical miner for thirty years and went on to appraise the mines at astronomical figures in full support of Butterfield's claims. But to his surprise an attorney for the *Financial News* stepped forward to subject him to a tedious and devastating cross examination, in which he finally admitted that only three of the properties could even be described as mines, that they were nowhere near worth the $5,000,000 asked and that they could not possibly pay a profit on that investment.

When news of the proceedings was telegraphed to London, the last hopes of the Homer District Consolidated Gold Mines, Ltd. collapsed. A suit to wind up the company was filed immediately and granted within a month. Butterfield had collected nearly $12,000 from stockholders, and he apparently had been living on this for three years; for when the company closed, its total assets were two shillings four pence. The following June, Butterfield lost his suit against the *Financial News* and his career in London was ended. Surprisingly, no action seems to have been taken against him. The West's leading mining journal, the San Francisco *Mining and Scientific Press*, also made no comment on the proceedings, but ran a series of articles on mining swindles, particularly those bilking the British. This ambiguous attitude suggests a policy of self-policing that kept well short of arrests.

During the examination Townsend's complicity in the fraud and his motives for reviving the *Homer Mining Index* appear to have come in for considerable criticism, and immediately upon his return to Lundy he lashed out at his attackers, forestalling further local comment from those who may have thought he sold out Lundy.

The editor of the INDEX has returned home after an absence of six weeks. Having suffered a severe surgical operation he is quite under the weather, but hopes to be in condition next week to pay his respects to the small-fry back-biters who have been talking with their mouths too much, and to the unclean beasts who have befouled their nests and reveled in the filth during his absence.

We want it distinctly understood that the INDEX has been supported and maintained solely and wholly by the individual efforts of its editor and proprietor. It has never seen the color of any other man's money except it was honestly earned. He who makes an assertion to the contrary is a venomous liar and loves malicious lying as a dog loves vomit. If we choose to publish a paper in Lundy it is nobody's business but our own, nor is it anybody's business if we have an object in view.

In his very denial, of course, Townsend had committed himself to continue the paper at Lundy as evidence that it was indeed run on its own. The following year, in fact, it may have become a paying proposition when Frederick Pike of Maine, the true owner of the May Lundy, and a San Francisco company with a lease on the Jackson and Lakeview, finally reopened the mines. But this could not yet be foreseen as the first snows began to fall in the winter of 1889—a winter whose severity throughout the West still remains unsurpassed.

14

Angular Sounds

THE WINTER of '89–'90 was one enormous unrelenting storm that held siege on all the western states for nearly five months. It brought rain, floods and snow to San Francisco, Sacramento and the Central Valley, while it blanketed the Sierra, the Great Basin, Oregon and Washington in a paralyzing blizzard. Trains were blockaded in the Sierra for many weeks at a time. The 600 passengers of a Southern Pacific train stranded in Reno were treated to their own newspaper, the *Snowbound*, issued by George McCully in January of 1890. Commerce was brought almost to a standstill in San Francisco and thousands lost their jobs; farms and crops were destroyed in the Central Valley; thousands of cattle froze to death in Nevada; farming and lumbering were halted in the Northwest and mining was completely paralyzed in the Sierra; cave-ins and floods severely damaged the underground workings of many mines, and avalanches destroyed a number of mills and surface works; many communities, including Lundy, were isolated without provisions or medical care; and through it all Jim Townsend composed some of his most vivid pieces.

The first snows fell in Lundy on the first day of November, and when Jim Townsend returned from San Francisco early in December the camp was already nearly buried beneath mountainous snow drifts. When at last the sun shone briefly into the canyon in January, some hoped that the storm was ending, but Jim lamented:

Last week we warned the people not to crow too soon. It must have been that somebody did prematurely chuckle over the momentary appearance of the sun last Saturday, for on Sunday the storm broke out again with quadrupled and multiplied violence. We thought that the combined genius of all the spiteful fiends in the nether regions could never devise anything more appallingly ferocious, but we changed our minds on Thursday, when a bitter blizzard swept down the canyon, compared with which all other blows were balmy zephyrs. At times it made the boldest man pale through the tinge of blue produced by cold. The air was filled with ice flying at a velocity of more than one hundred miles an hour, and nothing could be seen that was two feet distant. To compare it with an ordinary Winter storm would be like mistaking the gentle caresses of a child for premeditated murder. It was too tough to describe. It makes us smile tiredly to hear other people talk about difficulties encountered in the mountains during the Winter. Those complaining editors ought to take a peep into this canyon. They would quit whining and confess that the INDEX is published under almost inconceivable disadvantages and in the face of obstacles that would paralyze an ordinary man. Talk about looking around for news! Why we haven't been out of the house for two months nor can we get out.

And as the drifts deepened till the road down the canyon became "plugged up as tight as a bull's eye at fly time," Townsend wrote:

The grub question is getting to be a serious one. Many staple articles are either short or wholly consumed. Luxuries disappeared from our bill of fare long ago. The locker is nearly

empty, and no one can say when it will be replenished. And
still the storm keeps nagging us. These facts, taken raw, are not
palatable. If things don't change pretty soon we'll have to skip
out and inflict ourselves upon the ranchers at Mono Lake, who
at least have plenty of potatoes and live stock. But as it takes a
pretty good man to get down there, even on snowshoes, the old
men and cripples will have to be left behind to starve, unless
we eat them before we go.

But then new perils seized the camp as avalanches began to
sweep the great overburdens of snow on the surrounding peaks
down into the canyon. Townsend tried to record both the horror
and the grandeur of the scene, writing:

"A Night of Fearful Issue"
Hundreds of Snowslides
Tumbling from the Mountains

———

Becker's Lundy Brewery Demolished

———

The People of the Camp Await Disaster With Fear and Trembling . . .
Preparations to Abandon the Canyon
and Fly to the Valleys

Four months ago today the storm began, and, with a few intermissions of an hour or two each, has raged with unprecedented
violence ever since. Nothing like it was ever before experienced in these mountains or any other that we know of. At least
fifty feet of snow have fallen. In many places it is hundreds of
feet in depth. The sides of the mountains are overloaded, and
there is extreme danger from avalanches in every direction.

Last Saturday the camp was in high fever of fear. All day long
snowslides were tumbling and thundering, bringing down immense masses of rock and timber and piling them up into grotesque and fantastic mounds, some of which were of huge
dimensions. Everybody was nervously anxious, for disastrous
results seemed imminent. The gloomiest anticipations pre-
vailed. Both walls of the narrow canyon were covered with im-

mense banks of snow ready to fall and entomb us, and no one place appeared to be more secure than another.

In the morning a terrific slide came down from a deep gorge on the northern flank of Mount Gilcrest. Starting at a point about 3,000 feet above the town, it was augmented by slides from confluent canyons until its proportions were enormous, and with accelerated velocity it charged down the precipitous hill like a flood of molten silver. When it struck the lake there was a thundering crash of six-foot ice, followed instantly by cannon-like reports on the other side of the lake, as compressed air escaped from blow-holes in the ice. Some of these vents, however, emitted sounds like the hoarse roar of a steam fog-horn with a bad cold; others shrieked like seduced angels on the ragged edge of repentance and despair, while more seemed to howl with demonic glee over the wreck and ruin that threatened us.

For several minutes the air was filled with angular sounds punctuated by the cracking reports of artillery, as the ice was rent into great cakes and thrown in heaps along the margin of the lake. This diabolical fracas of clatter and smash was followed by silence that oppressed us like a nightmare. After a brief interval another slide started from the southern escarpment of Mt. Hector, on the opposite side of the lake. As it gathered material it accumulated speed, rolling over and over like breakers on a sloping shore and throwing feathery spray hundreds of yards ahead, until it shot out upon the lake like a flash and lay an inert mass of glittering white, akin to a glacier in solidity. The sight was weirdly and appallingly grand, so startling in its magnificence that the few beholders were prompted to kneel in adoration. It is at once awful and sublime to see a large slice of the earth in swift motion, but the sensation becomes one of abject fear when a person realizes the infinite danger that hovers in the track of one of these fascinating spectacles.

At noon of the same day there were two other slides, following each other in quick succession, converging at the lower ends so that they blended and became a single destroying monster. These started back of the Lundy brewery, and slid so noiselessly that our local beer factory looked like an italic almshouse before it was known that another avalanche had occurred. The large building was wiped out and spread out like soft butter upon hot bread. Its usefulness is no longer apparent, for it and its contents were ground into microscopic fragments. The valuable machinery and complete brewing apparatus are destroyed, entailing a great loss upon the proprietor, who is all the more unfortunate because of having expended a large sum of money in improvements during the year. The large cellar, filled with valuable stores and provisions, was supposed to have remained intact, but subsequent examination has proved that the whole outfit is crushed in. A rescue party tunneled into it and saved a good portion of the stores in fair condition. The double slide that wrecked Mr. Becker's property fortunately stopped a few feet short of the main building on the road, or that, too, would have been demolished. And it is also fortunate that Mr. Becker's cozy residence escaped, being but a short distance from the course of the avalanche.

Throughout the day slides were starting in all directions, and "Where will the next one come from?" was an oft-asked question. E. C. Green's house had a very close call. At one time it seemed to be booked for destruction, but the avalanche that threatened it was luckily deflected from its course by an intervening ridge.

The treacherous "Postoffice wash," which has been a menace for years, partially emptied itself to the great consternation of the people at the store. It was a vicious slide and had it come down with a full head on, would have gone clear across the canyon and demolished the May Lundy buildings, endangering a number of lives.

It was feared that the entire northern face of Gilcrest would drop its accumulations of snow and entomb the whole camp beyond resurrection, but fortunately the dreaded cataclysm did not occur. The white mantle of Scowden hung on tenaciously, except in a few places, much to our peace and comfort, else we would have had a more dismal story to relate today.

Toward night a gloom of distrust and foreboding settled upon us. The women and children were gathered at places that were presumed to be comparatively safe, while the men armed themselves with shovels and prepared for exigencies, with snowshoes and mufflers at hand. And so we anxiously awaited whatever might be in store for us. At Montrose's the fear and trembling of the people were allayed by the strains of Dandy Travis's fiddle, and they killed the gloomy night with song and dance, while the valiant "shovel brigade" was on the alert to give warning of disaster, but fortunately none occurred, though avalanches thundered all the time.

Next morning the falling snow turned to rain, and for three hours it came down in torrents. Then it became cold and the snow crusted with ice, which will make a fine bed for new snow to slide on. If we should have even a light fall now, with no wind, we may count on slides that will sweep the canyon from wall to wall, and they will come like eager lightning.

To be in readiness for an emergency, a number of large toboggans have been constructed, so that the women and children may be quickly removed to a place of safety when slides again threaten us. There seems to be no danger just now, but there is no telling what a day may bring forth. A snowslide is twin-devil to an earthquake, and gives no more warning. When it comes it comes "for keeps."

With this the majority of Lundy's scant population decamped for the valley below, leaving only Townsend and "another foolhardy person" behind. In fearless defiance of starvation and snowslides Lundy's last two inhabitants quickly looted the wood piles of those who had left. But as the storm pressed into its fifth month, Jim's wit became a little hard boiled.

The protracted tempestuousness is distracting. The edge of its novelty has worn off and we are ready to explode in disgust. And still the snow comes down, every flake a young avalanche. But we are in the habit of looking on the bright side of things and hope to get thawed out in time to hook onto the end of the procession at the resurrection. So let her snow and blow and be damned.

And she did. And the following week Jim was beside himself to find adjectives and superlatives enough to describe

The King of Storms

A Roaring Terror Raging From the Hills

A Sierra Cyclone on a Jamboree

The Camp Afflicted With Meteorological Jimjams

The Bile of Gospel Swampers Excited

Mountains of Lather and Droves of Waterspouts at Mono Lake

We are tired of talking about bad weather. Each storm that troops down upon us from the peaks and gorges of the snowy Sierras we consider to be infinitely worse than its immediate predecessor; and so it has been all through the Winter, coming wilder, fiercer and more devilish, one after another, with brief intermissions that serve only to render the contrast between fair and foul weather more marked and intolerable.

If there is a sensation beyond that of supreme disgust we are experiencing it right now. We thought that we knew something about mountain storms until last Monday, when we were compelled to confess that Old Boreas had more miserable things in his repertoire than we ever before dreamed of. If he keeps the best for the last, as they do at a puppet show, it is impossible to imagine what cruel terrors he has in store for us. We have experienced all conceivable forms of tempests in all quarters of the globe, but never anything approaching what we have been compelled to go through during the present week. At times it did not appear to be wind that came down the canyon in concentric circles. It was solid matter, consisting of rocks and ice flying with the velocity of light. Cannon-balls were slow in comparison. It was like a cyclone and a tornado running a foot-race. Houses and barns were picked up and distributed along the canyon in the shape of kindling-wood. In buildings that were strong enough to withstand the blast the windows were blown in, the doors had to be barricaded on the inside. Smoke-stacks and chimneys, early in the fray, went kiting toward the rising sun. It was pandemonium, bedlam and hell combined, a wreck and a crash in all directions, accompanied by noises that were appalling.

This fearful fracas maintained its grip throughout the ensuing night and day. Atrocious as it was it got worse on Tuesday evening, and threatened to twist the mountains out by the roots. No one could sleep during the night, and those who were fortunate enough to have cellars took refuge in them, and passed the night in constant expectation of seeing their houses start off schooner rig for Omaha.

Every house in camp became a cold, damp and miserable den. The wind penetrated every crack and crevice, driving in quantities of snow which soon melted and made things sloppy and cheerless. A man felt as if somebody were blowing up his trousers leg with a bellows and sketching the map of Greenland on the small of his back with an icicle. Snow collected within cloth ceilings, and deluged everything in the house. Pots and pans were in requisition to catch the innumerable drippings. Men swore and women almost cried with vexation. It made a fine opening for "la grippe," but none has appeared.

The INDEX office was in a fearful mess. Snow was from one to four feet deep all over it. The type cases were covered a foot deep, the "forms" on the "stone" were encased in ice six or eight inches in thickness, and the press looked like a way station on the Central Pacific. As fast as the snow was shoveled out it was blown back again. Then we sacked the confounded stuff and dumped it outside. In an instant it was a mile away. Next day there was the same old pile of snow inside. It came in through double windows and two-inch weather-boarding, covered with pasteboard and paper within. When we built a fire to warm things up and thaw them out, a thousand perpendicular rivulets started and drowned us out. It was a moist mess. Then we put the fire out, and everything froze solid as the rock of ages. The old printshop looked like a crystal grotto. It was not until yesterday that we could get to work on the paper. Its readers will this week get just what we choose to give them. If they don't like it, they can take their patronage elsewhere, as several political shrimps around here do.

The Postoffice store was in a sad plight on Tuesday morning. Mr. Butterfield asserts that he and his clerks shoveled out a hundred tons of snow. Such a condition of things never occurred before, though the building has stood the blasts of ten Winters without a leak. How the snow got in was not to be discovered, but there it was on everything, like frosting on a bridal cake, and ever so much thicker. Fortunately none of it got into the whisky. Snow-water is bad for the stomach.

On Monday Orrin Miller got as far as Hammond's Station with the mail, and could get no farther. Nate Miller, Otto Larsen and Indian Johnny wrestled with it and got it to the postoffice, being compelled, every few yards, to lie down and give the wind the right of way while crossing Lundy Lake, for nothing could stand against it. Orrin put his horse in Hammond's barn, and it took three men all that night and next day to dig him out, and two days more to make six miles on the return trip. Verily, the mail carrier in these hills has a dandy time in Winter.

Colonel Becker's residence was buried out of sight by a shifting drift of snow. He waited a long time for daylight, and at last consulted his watch and found that it was nearly noon and realized that he was entombed. A nice little tunnel, forty feet long, enabled him to see across the canyon once more.

Captain R. T. Pierce informs us that at Mono Lake everything was turned bottom up and topsy turvy. Thompson's house was up-ended, and now looks as if it had a brick chimney sticking out of a door, while what was a cellar wall seems to be a stone piazza, and the broadside has become the roof with half a dozen glassless skylights. A large haystack was picked up and dumped on top of Fraser's house, which is supposed to be under it in a state of smash. Miller's outdoor movables were taken out into the lake and dropped at intervals for several miles, and Fischer's goats have disappeared to the eastward. Judge Mattly's ranch was left in a mixed-up condition. Fences, barns and out-houses were done for in a twinkling and his cattle stampeded to the hills.

At the Deicas ranch the work of the storm was a great benefit, singular to say. Where there were ten feet of snow is now bare ground and cattle are browsing on the sagebrush.

The scene on the lake during the height of the storm was grand beyond anything ever before witnessed along the shores of the "Dead Sea of America." The water, which never freezes in the coldest weather, was lashed into foam by the furious wind, and into waves that would be no discredit to the Bay of Biscay or Cape Hatteras. Great mountains of lather, often miles in diameter, white as snow, would be formed as if by magic, and as quickly whisked away before the gale. All day long, fleets of these phantom ships were sailing across the lake in ghostly procession, to be stranded on the eastern shore, a sight at once grand and beautiful.

In the wake of these weird craft immense columns of water would be lifted by whirlwinds to the heights of hundreds of feet, rising like a freed balloon, to a level above the plane of the storm, as it seemed, where it would be churned into lather and dissipated into invisible spray. Despite the raging storm, it was the most magnificent exhibition that phlegmatic Gospel Swampers ever witnessed. They will probably now confess that there are grander things than ponderous spuds and ten-horse power garlic.

But this was the final encore—the storm at last had ended! The following month the town dug out on its annual Resurrection Day, and a chastened and weary Jim Townsend set out to establish a truly self-sustaining paper at Lundy. If the strain of the mining investigation and the rigors of the Big Winter did not break both his spirit and his health, this last task did, and in one waning decade "Lying Jim" Townsend became a memory.

15

Greased for the Occasion

WHEN A MAN begins to slide down hill he finds everything greased for the occasion," Jim Townsend often wrote, adding also that "when he tries to climb up he finds everything greased for the occasion too." In his last years he found that the going was also greased for those who merely wanted to hang on. For although the Lundy mines had reopened, their output was small and the fare for the journalist was thin indeed. As a result Jim was willing to take subscribers or advertisers on any terms, offering: "Wild or tame ducks, chickens, cordwood or money taken for subscriptions to the INDEX. Also old clothes and cathartic pills." When the few new readers attracted by this fell arrears in their payment, Townsend sought to woo them with verse:

> The wind bloweth; the water floweth;
> The farmer soweth; the subscriber oweth;
> And the Lord knoweth that we are in need of our dues;
> So come a runnin', ere we go gunnin'—we're not a funnin';
> This thing of dunnin' gives us the everlastin' blues.

Now ill health began to plague him almost constantly, many times making him barely able to get out the paper—even as a half sheet. Willing to try anything for relief, for several weeks he even tried advertising: "A complete outfit of pains, aches, rheumatism and general debility for sale. Apply this office. Any person desiring to cultivate irascibility will do well to examine the goods."

But he found more comfort in the bottle, and, as a result, the profusion of humorous quips and vignettes that once brought life to the pages of the *Index* became rarer and rarer. Only occasionally did he write an item reminiscent of the genius he once displayed—one surviving tale, "A Singular Freak," written in 1894 still captures this spirit.

While S. B. Burkham was on his way to Lundy the other day he met with a singular as well as laughable incident. As he was jogging along the road he met a man on the dead run who looked at him with pleading eyes as he shot by and agonizingly shrieked, "Stop me, for God's sake!" and away he flew in a flame of dust. Burkham noticed that the fellow's face was covered with dust and sweat, and thinking that the fleeing fugitive might be propelled by some occult force—or perhaps a flock of hornets in the slack of his breeches—he turned his horse and gave chase. He could still hear a wild cry for help. The man was a sprinter but Burkham soon overhauled him. "Stop me! Stop me!" "Stop yourself, you d——d fool!" retorted Burkham. "I can't!" howled the flyer in a despairing voice. Then Burkham drove up alongside and seized him, when he fell in an inanimate heap, apparently dead with exhaustion. A generous jolt of whisky revived him sufficiently to enable him to state the cause of his singular conduct. He said he was afflicted with a sort of nervous paralysis. When one of the spells came on he lost all control of his legs and they ran away with him. He usually carried a halter with which to hitch himself, but he had carelessly left it in camp the night before. "How far did you come at that gait?" asked Burkham. "I don't know how far it is," was the response, "but I came through Mammoth about daylight this morning—been going all night like a train of cars." "Good

Lord!" ejaculated the astounded Postmaster, "you have come more than 100 miles." "That's nothing for me," said the freak. "I would have done it quicker, but down here a piece one leg went faster than the other, so that I had to run around in a circle for about four hours. I was pretty well tuckered out, and if you hadn't stopped me I'd have run back to camp again. Much obliged to you for stopping me. But you'll never catch me out again without a halter." Burkham suggested that it would be better for him to go hobbled all the time, and rode off, wondering how the freak could be utilized.

But most of the time Jim lounged in Charley Taylor's Lakeview Saloon, reflecting contentedly, "by the time a man is old enough to realize what a lot he does not know, he is too old to worry over it, and when he has lost his enthusiasm he begins to enjoy things. That's why we are happy in these mountains."

As the years dragged out, Jim's failing health forced him to the Bay a number of times for medical care. There he sought out old friends with whom to make the cocktail route and share his flickering wit. Bob Davis, then editor of the San Francisco literary and gossip magazine *Chic*, preserved one of the last of these conversations in 1895.

A Chat With The Liar Of Lundy

There is a newspaper man in Nevada by the name of Jim Townsend who occasionally comes to San Francisco. He is here now. I met him on Montgomery street the other day, and with his usual happy expression he handed me a cigar and asked if I could steer him to the home of some capitalist.

"I have a scheme that will bust the Salt Lake egg market wide open, but it takes capital to get the thing started. Just show me a capitalist and in ten minutes I will have him soaking his watch to get the money needed to begin!"

"What is your scheme, Jim?" I inquired.

"I'll tell you in a few words. It is simply to get seven acres of ground out in the wilderness and stock it with chickens. Come off to one side I don't want anyone to hear this. Well after you get your chickens, some several thousands, why have a lot of nests made with trap doors in the bottom—doors that open and let the eggs drop through as soon as they are laid. Of course you know a chicken likes to advertise such an accomplishment, and will glance around to view the work before beginning to cackle. Ah, there's where you get in your work! The egg will have disappeared and the hen will have to get to work and lay another. I figure that a conscientious hen will lay about five eggs before throwing up the job, and there you are. Where's your capitalist?"

I informed him that since it was found practicable to cross Plymouth Rock chickens with Klamath River salmon and lay 800 eggs a week that his scheme would probably fall through.

"Well," he answered, "then let's build a flying machine. I can show a man of sense how it is practicable to put up a working model that will illustrate the possibilities of my plan."

"How much money do you want, Jim?"

"Oh, about $300,000 to start with. It will be perpetual motion, also."

"About $300,000? What will be the size of it?"

"About a mile long," he replied, stroking his chin complacently, "and it will be the hardest thing to stop (when it gets started) you ever saw. Really you will have to begin stopping half an hour before it starts. It's the fastest thing you ever saw and will get to the next town three days before the old woman's gossip."

When I expressed surprise about the size of the model and asked how large he proposed to make the real machine, his reply was:

"When the nose is coming into San Francisco the tail end will be pulling out of Chicago. We don't want to crowd the seating capacity, and it's also well to have plenty of advertising space. Can you put me onto a man who has brains as well as money?"

His entire life is made up of such anecdotes and at a moment's notice he is ready to lie.

Davis then recalled,

On one occasion Townsend was a witness in a mining case tried in this city.

"How high is Lundy, Mr. Townsend?" asked an attorney.

"It's the highest town on the Coast. Beer is $2 a bottle."

"I mean the altitude, sir," answered the lawyer somewhat tartly.

"Oh, I see. Well, most people don't believe it, but at times you can look over the moon and the hills are so steep that sunshine rolls off the sides and lays at the foot of the slopes in big folds. On a real bright day it plugs up the streets and stops travel."

By 1895 Townsend was no longer able to manage the paper himself in Lundy, and in October he suspended the *Homer Mining Index* for the last time to move it to Bodie, where a little prosperity might allow him to employ help. Dan Jones had stopped printing the Bodie *Evening Miner* in the spring of 1891 and had set to drift again, winding up in Sacramento. The *Miner* plant stood idle for only a few months, however, before it was revived by an enthusiastic young printer named A. V. Morgan. A few years robbed him of his enthusiasm, and 1895 found the paper with boiler plate outsides in the hands of R. L. McCarthy.

Jim took several months to haul the *Index* plant over from Lundy, and it was not until four days before Christmas that he finally issued his first paper in Bodie, as simply *The Mining Index*. The format was the same as the Lundy paper with nearly all the old ads remaining from Lundy plus a few new ones from Bodie—but its spirit was gone. His unsteady and arthritic hands prevented him from holding the compositor's stick and a failing back could not bear the presswork, so he was forced to hire two girls, Idell and Christine Gregory, to set the type and pay a hunchback derelict to pull the press for him once a week. Nonetheless the paper paid its way, and Townsend was able to buy out McCarthy in December of 1896 and combine the two papers as the *Miner-Index*.

George Montrose, who occasionally helped around the printing office at this time, preserved the last fading image of Lying Jim. "Jim was a tall, slim man, grizzled and gray, when I knew him. His hair was long and frowsy; his mustache long and rather bushy and trained to point down both sides of his mouth. He generally wore a well-worn and greenish tinged-with-age Prince

Albert coat; his pants unpressed and knees baggy with age and not from prayers; a paper collar and a black string tie; his shoes were strangers to blackening; and a well-worn and crumpled soft black hat completed his attire. He was a heavy drinking man and seldom was what you would call really sober."

But even freed of the physical burdens of the printing shop and liberated from all other cares by the balm of Judge Maestretti's spirits, Jim found no relief from the bitter winters, and his health continued to slip away. Four more winters took a heavy toll upon him, convincing him at last that he could continue no longer. Thus before the snow fell again he sold the paper and bid a final adieu to Bodie, printing, mining and the Sierra.

I am old and crippled with gout besides being tired of conducting a newspaper single-handed. Therefore, in mercy to myself, I have disposed of the MINER-INDEX to the Misses Gregory and shall take a rest. They should be supported by the people as they deserve to be. There is a field here for bright young ladies.

Sept. 30, 1899   J. W. E. Townsend

Jim spent that winter with friends in Oakland and dreamed of writing an autobiography, which he planned to entitle *Truth With Variations*. But with eyesight and health failing rapidly, he went east the following summer to spend his last weeks with his older brother in Lake Forrest, Illinois. There he died on August 11, 1900, at the age of 62 years and 7 days.

16

Epilogue:
A Field for Bright Young
Ladies

WHEN NEWS of Lying Jim Townsend's death reached the West Coast it received notice, and in many cases generous attention, in every newspaper from San Francisco to Virginia City. From among the many obituaries, we quote portions of one of the more accurate, in implication if not in fact—the one written by Allen Bragg for the Reno *Evening Gazette* of August 23.

ANOTHER OF THE OLD-TIME JOURNALISTS
GONE TO HIS REWARD.

At Lake Forest, Ill., August 10th, Captain J. W. E. Townsend, the best all-around newspaperman of the Pacific coast, balanced up the books in this world and has gone to another, where, if the theory of evolution is a correct one, he will open up another set and keep right on. Jim Townsend was in many respects a wonderful man, and one of the best all-around printers and newspaper men on this coast. He had a great big, generous heart, and was so full of good nature and wit as a nut is of meat.

He came to this coast early in the fifties, and for many years was the foreman in the old Sacramento *Union* office when it was the leading paper on the coast. He could go to the "case," and, without copy, set up a paragraph that would make a horse laugh; or, if cynically inclined, he could set up a paragraph that would cut to the heart.

Mr. Townsend was employed on the *Gazette* by R. L. Fulton when he owned the paper, and, like the present editor, was an employee. After Townsend came to work on the *Gazette* we soon became very intimate with him, and the intimacy soon ripened into a deep-rooted friendship which has lasted to the end, and a memory left of a noble fellow whose every heart pulsation was of the most generous. He would divide with a friend any day and anywhere, and under any circumstance. Even the mule he used to ride while prospecting years ago he would divide with.

The *Gazette* man remembers receiving a telegram from Townsend to meet him at the Virginia & Truckee train at the time he was publishing the Luning [*sic*] paper and he had been in his mountain fastness for several years. We met him, and, as was ever Jim's custom whenever an opportunity presented, we "took something." He invited us over the street to renew those pleasant recollections of long ago. As we crossed over and were about the middle of the street we stopped to talk. Jim was badly crippled up with rheumatism at the time, and walked with a cane, while one foot was encased in a big carpet slipper. While we were talking someone skipped past us on a bicycle. Jim jumped, and, catching us by the arm, said:

"Who the hell was that on the nickel-plated jackass?"

Had he made the best use of his wit and talents he might have been one of the great men of the age, but, like the rest of us, he did not, being satisfied to publish a paper in some little mountain town where he could work up a good "cocktail route."

But a truer friend and a man with more noble impulses never lived than J. W. E. Townsend.

Farewell, old friend, farewell. Your pungent paragraphs in coast journalism will keep your memory green for many years. May your slumbers be all blessed.

Over the next decade, Townsend's fellow editors continued to recall his memory and reminisce about his contribution to their trade. Out of all these, as a final fitting tribute, we offer a part of that written by another frontier news-and-confidence man, "George Graham Rice." Born Jacob Simon Herzig in New York, Rice began his nefarious career by stealing from his father to pay gambling debts. He graduated from Reform School to Sing Sing, went on to publishing racing tipsheets and wound up running an "advertising agency" in the Goldfield-Tonopah region in 1904, touting spurious mines. But he was a charmer, and knew another when he heard of one. He devoted much of his "By-the-Bye" column in his *Nevada Mining News* for August 27, 1908, to retailing some Townsend anecdotes collected here and there and concludes with an interesting project.

"There was never any question but that the most versatile liar that the Coast ever produced was Jim Townsend, who ran the Mono *Index* for years," said James P. Kennedy, the Comstock litterateur in the course of talk at the Hotel Reno roof-garden last evening. "He was full of originality of expression and ready wit, and it was really a pleasure to sit down and listen to his bubbling fund of anecdote and interesting reminiscences, most of which he manufactured as he went along. . . . As a rule half the papers on the Coast selected a half column or so of 'Townsendisms,' and they were copied all over the Union. It seems a pity that the back files of this remarkable sheet could not be rescued and a compilation made of them. Such a collection would be a classic in the way of original Nevada humor!"

As partisans, we hope to be forgiven our agreement.

And as students of the continuing reverberations of the past, we offer a concluding curiosity. In 1955, Professor William H.

Behle of the Biology Division of the University of Utah published a note in the journal *Bird-Banding* in which he expressed great interest in coming across one of the earliest records of banding in literature, as well as an extreme longevity record. The item was taken by J. Cecil Alter from *The Millenial Star* (June 25, 1894, p. 416). The story had in turn been taken from the Territorial papers but with no indication of which one or the date. It ran:

A wild goose has been captured west of the Utah line. Attached to the bird's leg was a very thin piece of brass, an inch long and half as wide. On this is punched with a pointed instrument, "Fremont Party, September, 1846, B. B. J." It is presumed that the initials are those of Colonel B. B. Jackson, who was a member of Fremont's exploring expedition when it passed through the region nearly fifty years ago. The venerable colonel is living somewhere in Sonoma County, California, and has been informed of the capture. If he remembers having turned a tagged goose loose in 1846 the bird will be presented to the California Pioneer Society."

This improbable item puzzled both Professor Behle and E. Alexander Bergstrom, editor of *Bird-Banding*, for the obvious reasons and sent them on a wild chase—for mention of a gift goose—through Fremont's reports, the records of the Society of California Pioneers, the surviving notices of Colonel Jackson in the Society's volume marked "Bodie," and, finally, a page-by-page search of possible source newspapers for the item. At last it was found in the *Deseret Evening News* for May 24, 1894, p. 8, with some additional information. An introductory sentence read, "James H. Sturgeon captured a wild goose at his place one day last week, and he thinks that he has a grand prize," and at the end, the ultimate source for the item: "Homer (Nev.) *Index*." Although the professor succeeded in unraveling the hoax, it does go to show the mischievous persistence of the wit aroused by wilderness.

Glossary

alley   the floor space between two rows of compositors' stands

antimony   a brittle metal used in type alloys

Babbitt metal   an antifriction alloy for lining bearings

blanket   see *tympan*

boiler plate   syndicated material supplied to weekly papers in plate form (rather than in "standing type," from which news stories were printed)

case   a shallow tray divided into boxes for holding type characters, one typeface or font to each tray

chase   a rectangular steel (earlier, wooden) frame into which type is locked for positioning on the bed of the press for printing

compositor   a person who sets type for printing

copying press   a device in which an original in copying ink is transferred by being pressed against an absorbent translucent sheet which is read from the reverse side

deadstone   see *imposing stone*

devil   a young apprentice (often black with ink) in a printing office

distribute   to break up lines or pages of type, restoring each character to its proper box in the job case

em   a unit of measure of type; a common-size spacer or "quad"

exchanges   agreements between newspapers to reprint each other's material

form   the combination of letterpress material imposed and locked up in a chase with the furniture, quoins, and the chase itself

frame   see *chase*

galley   an oblong tray with upright sides to hold set type

imposing stone   a slab on which type is arranged and locked into frames preparatory to printing

masthead   the nameplate of a newspaper, often with information about its publication

pi, pied   spilled, mixed, or incorrectly distributed type; chaos

quoins   metal or wooden wedges used to lock up type in a chase or galley

rollers   revolving cylinders for inking faces of type on the press

salutatory   an inaugural editorial

tympan   a sheet of buffer material placed behind the paper to be printed

typesetter's stick   a shallow tray having an adjustable slide that is held in one hand by a compositor as he sets type in it with the other

typos   typographers or compositors

valedictory   a final editorial

MINING

arrastra   a crude circular stone mill within which a stone is dragged to pulverize ores

assessment   a demand upon shareholders for money, usually to raise working capital

color   small particles of gold in a miner's pan after the waste has been washed away

crosscut   a mine working driven at right angles to a drift or orebody

drift   a nearly horizontal mine passage driven on or parallel to the
  course of a vein

flume   an inclined channel for conveying water

quicksilver   mercury, used in amalgamating ores

tailings   a slope formed by an accumulation of mining waste

talus   a natural slope formed by an accumulation of falling rock

Acknowledgments

THE AUTHORS would like to express their gratitude to all who helped us collect Jim Townsend's writing and research his life. In particular we thank the staffs of the Bancroft Library, Berkeley; the Library of the California Historical Society, San Francisco; the Nevada Historical Society, Reno; the California State Library, Sacramento; the Nevada State Library, Carson City; and the New Hampshire Historical Society, Concord, for their kind cooperation. We are also indebted to Ella M. Cain of Bridgeport, David F. Myrick of San Francisco, Cecil G. Tilton of Moraga, Marvyn Wittelle of Lake Forrest, Illinois, J. Hilary Cook of Turlock, Oliver J. Kirkpatrick of Palm Springs, Charles A. Lundy of Blairsden, Mrs. George A. Montrose of Gardnerville, and Idell Gregory Sherwin of Mountain View for searching their notes, family papers, and memories for material on Lying Jim.

In the libraries mentioned above lie the primary materials for this volume: the files of early Nevada and California newspapers, the published reminiscences of western writers and the studies of those writers. Following is a list of the sources consulted, together with the symbols used in referring to the most important of them in the notes.

Sources

Angels Camp, California, *Mountain Echo*.

AL   Antioch, California, *Ledger*.

Aurora, Nevada, *Esmeralda Herald*.

Benton, California, *Tri-Weekly Letter*.

Benton, California, *Bentonian*.

Bodie, California, *Bodie Evening Miner*.

BFP   Bodie, California, *Daily Free Press*.

Bodie, California, *Miner-Index*.

BSN   Bodie, California, *Weekly Standard News*.

Carson City, Nevada, *Daily Index*.

MA   Carson City, Nevada, *Morning Appeal*.

Drury, Wells. *An Editor on the Comstock Lode*. New York: Farrar and Rinehart, 1936.

Fulton, Robert L. "Bret Harte and Truthful James." *Overland Monthly* (August 1915): 89–98.

Gillis, William R. *Gold Rush Days with Mark Twain*. New York: Albert and Charles Boni, 1930.

Graham, Jared B. *Handset Reminiscences*. Salt Lake: Century Publishing, 1915.

Hawthorne, Nevada, *Oasis*.

Linder, Howard K. "Dean of the Mining Camp Journalists." *Desert Magazine* (September 1961): 26–29.

London, *Financial News*.

London, *Times*.

HMI   Lundy, California, *Homer Mining Index*.

Mack, Effie Mona. *Nevada*. Glendale: Arthur H. Clarke, 1936.

Montrose, George A. "'Lying Jim', or 'Truthful James' of the High Sierra." *The Pony Express* (November 1952): 3–7.

Nevada City, California, *Nevada Daily Gazette*.

REG   Reno, Nevada, *Evening Gazette*.

San Francisco, California, *Chic*.

San Francisco, California, *Examiner*.

San Francisco, California, *Mid-Winter Appeal*.

TI   Sonora, California, *Tuolumne Independent*.

TE   Virginia City, Nevada, *Territorial Enterprise*.

VEC   Virginia City, Nevada, *Evening Chronicle*.

Notes

1 / INTRODUCTION

Extensive bibliographies on American humor can be found in the books by Blair and Hill. Of special relevance to the West are F. L. Pattee, "The Laughter of the West," in *American Literature Since 1870* (New York, 1915), pp. 25–44; Mody Boatright, *Folk Laughter on the American Frontier* (New York, 1949); Franklin D. Walker, *San Francisco's Literary Frontier*, rev. ed. (Seattle, 1969), and *The Frontier Humorists: Critical Views*, ed. M. Thomas Inge (Athens, Ga., 1975). Of the dozens of relevant studies on Twain, we will cite only H. N. Smith, ed., *Mark Twain of the Enterprise* (Berkeley, 1957), Paul Fatout, *Mark Twain in Virginia City* (Bloomington, 1964), and David E. E. Sloan, *Mark Twain as a Literary Comedian* (Baton Rouge, 1979). For the other writers listed, see, for example, Linda D. Barnet, *Bret Harte: A Reference Guide* (Boston, 1980); David M. Goodman, *A Western Panorama* (Glendale, 1966); George R.

Stewart, *John Phoenix Esquire* (New York, 1937); Richard G.
Lillard, "Dan De Quille, Comstock Reporter and Humorist,"
Pacific Historical Review, 13 (1944): 251–59; Fred H. Hart, *The
Sazerac Lying Club*, 5th ed. (San Francisco, 1878); David B.
Kesterson, *Bill Nye: The Western Writings* (Boise, 1976).

2 / King of the Cannibal Islands

Townsend's arrival in San Francisco is recalled by Joe Goodman,
San Francisco, *Mid-Winter Appeal*, 21 January 1894. Although
no direct record of Townsend's birth has been found, his death
certificate, filled out from the statements of his brother and
filed in the Lake County Recorder's Office, Waukegan, Illinois,
shows him to have been 62 years, 7 days old at his death on 11
August 1900. This is corroborated by the Census Report for
1850 of the "free inhabitants" of Portsmouth, New Hampshire.
Jim's reminiscence is from AL, 27 August 1870. His Fiji Islands
exploits are related in Jared B. Graham, *Handset Reminiscences*, pp. 171–73. Gillis quote from *Gold Rush Days With
Mark Twain*, pp. 181–210. "Truthful James" is discussed in
Gillis, pp. 181–82; in the Robert Fulton article; and in Wells
Drury, *An Editor on the Comstock Lode*, pp. 197–98. Richard
O'Connor's views from *Bret Harte: A Biography* (Boston, 1966),
pp. 120–21. The San Francisco *Mirror* story is told by Graham,
pp. 102–3, 167–70.

3 / Dirty Scamp and Miscreant

Jim's Virginia City description, REG, 2 May 1882. Townsend
and Twain on the *Enterprise*, J. Wells Kelly, *Second Directory
of the Nevada Territory 1863* (San Francisco, 1863). Authorship
of the "Jumping Frog" claimed for Jim in REG, 23 August 1900;
TE, 23 August 1900; VEC, 23 August 1900; REG 20 June 1933;
and Effie Mona Mack, *Nevada* (Glendale, 1936), p. 454. The
story appears in the Sonora *Herald*, 11 June 1853; see Oscar
Lewis, *The Origin of the Celebrated Jumping Frog of Calaveras
County* (San Francisco, 1931). Jim's activities on the Grass Valley
Union treated in the Nevada City, *Nevada Daily Gazette*, 29
October to 7 November 1864, and Fulton. Marriage to Eliza-
beth J. Lindsey recorded in the Lyon County Recorder's Office,

Yerington, Nevada. His views of San Francisco newspaperwork, AL, 6 August 1870.

4 / HOG-REEVE
Description of Antioch, AL, 22 October 1870. "Who Wants a Mosquito Ranch," AL, 23 July 1870. "Hog-Reeve," AL, 27 August 1870. "Dead-Hogs—Ugh!" AL, 6 August 1870. A subscriber quits AL, 23 July 1870. "A Rat," AL, 9 July 1870. "The Vicissitudes of Bachelor Life," AL, 30 April 1870. "A Steam Vaquero," AL, 25 June 1870. "A Bed-bug Story," AL, 17 September 1870. Jim sells out, AL, 8 April 1871.

5 / THE CHEESE PRESS
The cheese press, Benton, *Tri-Weekly Letter*, 7 June 1879. Dan Jones's diet, Benton, *Bentonian*, 14 February 1880. His copying press, ibid., 29 September 1880. "Toll Roads," ibid., 21 August 1879. His credo and his plight, ibid., 29 September 1880. Jim Townsend's arrival, Aurora, *Esmeralda Herald*, 8 May 1880.

6 / BRASS MINERS
Jim's arrival in Lundy, HMI, 12 June 1880. "A Rough Country," and "Pouring In," HMI, 26 June 1880. Epigrams, HMI, 19 and 26, June 1880. "A Social Cloudburst," HMI, 19 June 1880. "The Sly Woodtick," HMI, 26 June 1880. "The Glorious Fourth," HMI, 3 July 1880. "Curry's Brass Mine," HMI, 4 December 1880. "A Mill Creek Goat," HMI, 27 November 1880. "The Tables Turned," HMI, 4 December 1880. "Our New Barber," HMI, 18 December 1880.

7 / TOE JAM AND BULL BUTTER
A Lundy zephyr, *Esmeralda Herald*, 29 January 1881. The hotel wreck, HMI, 9 April 1881. "Hard Times in Lundy," HMI, 11 December 1880. The *Index* office, HMI, 18 December 1880. Jim's salutatory, HMI, 1 January 1881. The court room, ibid. "A Remarkable Case," HMI, 27 November 1880. "An Absorbing Trespass Case," HMI, 29 January 1881. "An Interesting Trial," HMI, 26 February 1881. "They Quit the Use of Tobacco," HMI, 19 February 1881. "The Dusenberry Reform Club," HMI, 19

March 1881. Jim's cure, HMI, 23 April 1881. "Washington's Birthday," HMI, 26 February 1881. "Bull Teaming," HMI, 22 January 1881. "Wilcox's Pig," HMI, 19 March 1881. "Whoopee!," HMI, 19 February 1881.

8 / ROUND MEN IN SQUARE HOLES

"A Phenomenal Storm," HMI, 25 March 1881. "Burkham's Circus," HMI, 29 October 1881. Jim's silence, BFP, 7 July 1881. "No Place for a Cat," BSN, 19 October 1881. Dan Jones's valedictory, Hawthorne, *Oasis*, 6 October 1881 quoted in BFP, 7 October 1881. Round men in square holes, TE, quoted in BSN, 4 January 1882. Barnes's raid, BFP, 2 August 1882.

9 / THE NEW BOSS LIAR OF THE UNIVERSE

Jim in the Mother Lode, Angels Camp, *Mountain Echo*, 21 March 1882. Richard C. Datin, in "A Wilde Time in Nevada," *The Nevadan* (October 1980), pp. 5, 32, attributes to Townsend an anonymous story that appeared in Fulton's *Reno Evening Gazette* concerning a stopover made by Oscar Wilde during his American tour, 25 March 1882. "Hoggishness," REG, 14 May 1882. "A Boston Female," REG, 15 June 1882. "You Can't Fool Them," REG, 19 May 1882. "The Bold Ben Gets Sold," REG, 22 May 1882. "A Pugnacious Touress," REG, 2 May 1882. "Eli Perkins," REG, 20 May 1882. See Melville D. Landon, *Eli Perkins: Thirty Years of Wit, and Reminiscences of Witty, Wise, and Eloquent Men* (New York, 1891). Jim and the Marquis of Lorne, BFP, 15 and 17 September 1882. "Sweet Scented Brakemen," REG, 14 May 1882. "A Case of Sheep-Jiggles," REG, 24 May 1882. "A Piute Giantess," REG, 13 May 1882. "Dancing," REG, 10 June 1882. "Scared to Death," REG, 13 May 1882. "The Mortuary Artist," REG, 3 June 1882. Jim's arrastras, HMI, 24 June to 15 July 1882.

10 / FOURTEEN CATS IN FIFTEEN MINUTES

Two tales of Jackson, BSN, 19 July 1882, and BFP, 8 August 1882. "An Accommodating Court," HMI, 10 November 1883. "His Third Death," HMI, 27 October 1883. A "biographical" sketch, VEC quoted in HMI, 27 May 1882. Jim's inheritance, BFP, 3 June 1882. "Jim Townsend Ruined," HMI, 6 September 1884. Jim in Virginia City, VEC, 26 May 1884. Old Boreas, TE, 17 October 1886. The *Daily Index* salutatory, in that paper, 25 December 1886, along with "A Queer Experience."

11 / A Hole in the Ground
"O. Seim," HMI, 19 January 1884. Dan Jones's counterblast, Bodie, *Bodie Evening Miner,* 18 March 1889. Marriott's expose, San Francisco, *News-Letter* quoted in London, *The Times,* 10 June 1890, and San Francisco, *News-Letter,* 27 October 1887 quoted in London, *Financial News,* 8 November 1887.

12 / Resurrection
The revival of the *Homer Mining Index,* MA, 30 October 1888. Jim's mining report, HMI, 17 August 1889. "J. W. Heilshorn," HMI quoted in VEC, 1 October 1889. More saloons, HMI quoted in TI, 14 May 1892. Coyote lode-line, HMI, 1 February 1890. "A Man Named Quinn," HMI, 11 November 1893. "A Screaching Blizzard," HMI, 11 May 1889 quoted in MA, 16 May 1889. Trapped indoors, HMI, quoted in TI, 23 January 1892. "Resurrection" ad, HMI, 30 March 1889 quoted in MA, 2 April 1889. "Resurrection Day," HMI, 6 April 1889 quoted in VEC, 10 April 1889. A lot of truck, HMI, quoted in MA, 8 March 1891. "A Mono Lake Monster," HMI, 26 January 1889 quoted in VEC, 30 January 1889. "A Mystery Solved," HMI, 25 May 1889 quoted in VEC 28 May 1889. "Dancing Boulders," HMI, 2 August 1890 quoted in VEC, 6 August 1890. "A Sleep-Walker's Wealth," HMI, 17 August 1889. "My Friend the Editor," San Francisco, *Examiner,* 21 July 1889.

13 / The Talking Machine of Lundy
Jim on the road, HMI, 2 November 1889 quoted in VEC, 6 November 1889. "Jim Townsend in Carson," MA, 30 October 1889. The Big Hole Mine, MA, 23 November 1889. Jim at the Palace, MA, 6 December 1889. The true worth of the mines, VEC, 18 November 1889. The company's assets, London, *The Times,* 16

December 1889. The end of Butterfield, ibid., 10 and 13 June 1890. Jim's indignant note, HMI, 14 December 1889 quoted in MA, 19 December 1889.

14 / ANGULAR SOUNDS

Jim's lament, HMI, 25 January 1890 quoted in MA, 5 February 1890. "The Grub Question," HMI, 1 February 1890. "A Night of Fearful Issue," HMI, 1 February 1890. "Protracted Tempestuousness," HMI, quoted in VEC, 3 March 1890. "The King of Storms," HMI, 1 March 1890.

15 / GREASED FOR THE OCCASION

"Down Hill," HMI, 9 April 1881, and Bodie, *Mining Index*, 15 May 1896 quoted in VEC, 18 May 1896. "Wild and tame ducks," HMI, quoted in MA, 29 October 1891. Poem, HMI, 19 November 1892 quoted in VEC, 23 November 1892. "A complete outfit of pains," HMI, quoted in TI, 28 November 1891. "A Singular Freak," HMI, 26 May 1894. "Old enough," HMI, quoted in TI, 30 April 1892. "A Chat with the Liar of Lundy," San Francisco, *Chic*, 15 January 1895, pp. 6–7. George Montrose's description of Jim, George A. Montrose, "'Lying Jim', or 'Truthful James' of the High Sierra," Placerville, *The Pony Express*, November 1952, pp. 3–7. Townsend's valedictory, Bodie, *Miner-Index*, 30 September 1899, clipping in Alf Doten's diary, 5 October 1899, in the collection of the University of Nevada, Reno.

16 / EPILOGUE

Obituary quote, REG, 23 August 1900. Rice quote, *Nevada Mining News*, 27 August 1908. Bird-Banding hoax, William H. Behle, "A Supposed Bird Banding in the Great Basin in 1846," *Bird-Banding* 26 (1955), 117–18.

Index